Contents

WITHDRAWN

Acknowledgements

We are very grateful to the following people for giving us feedback on the first draft of this book: Neil Galloway, Dave Hewett, Gren Knight, Claire Marvin, Beryl Smith, Carol Ouvry and Christina Tilstone. We also thank Valerie Farnworth for typing, proofreading and feedback; and Noreen Stacey for typing.

Introduction

The Central Aims of this Text

- *To present a summary of interactive approaches to teaching and learning.*
- *To enable teachers to re-evaluate their basic teaching methods in the light of interactive approaches.*
- *To provide a means by which teachers of students with learning difficulties can investigate and experiment with interactive approaches.*

There is an attempt to pull together the material which is at present scattered amongst the literature and is largely inaccessible to practising teachers. This has been presented in a fashion which we anticipate can have a direct impact on teaching practice.

The Audience

Throughout the text, an emphasis has been placed on accessing interactive approaches to teaching to the widest audience. To this end we have aimed to be as jargon-free as possible and to make as few assumptions as possible about the background and qualifications of the reader or course participant.

The book will be of particular interest to teachers in schools and lecturers in further and higher education; but it is also designed to interest other related professionals, such as learning disability nurses, support workers, occupational therapists and speech therapists. It is also hoped that parents will find it useful.

We pondered about the use of appropriate vocabulary, fearful that some terminology might convey inappropriate messages or simply put readers off. In an effort to meet these concerns the term 'student' or 'learner' has been used throughout to indicate that interactive approaches should not be tied to any one age group, or type of learning difficulty. The term 'teacher' is used throughout and is taken to imply anyone with a teaching role. We have also, for convenience sake, referred to the classroom on several occasions, though it should be stressed that this should not be taken to restrict the environments in which it may be used. Interactive approaches are widely applicable.

Theory to practice In the 1970s and early 1980s behavioural theory provided an effective framework for the teaching of children with a variety of learning difficulties. It was effective in that the theory was directly related to, and informed by practice. Teachers could use behavioural theory on Monday morning. It provided them with security in the knowledge that they were armed with a set of justifications for what they were doing on a daily basis. A more sceptical view would be that it provided teachers with the belief that they were 'specialists' just at a time when they needed this confidence. Most important of all it apparently worked. Teachers were able to change something in their students in a consistent way. There was most definitely a 'feeling of optimism in the air' (Smith, 1989). The 1971 Education Act established the principle that no child was ineducable, a point many had fought long and hard to enshrine in law. Now teachers were under pressure to provide evidence for this principle in their day-to-day work with such pupils.

Behavioural practice was disseminated in a thoroughly digestible way through such tools as the EDY (Education of the Developmentally Young) course (Foxen and McBrien, 1981) and the TASS project (Robson, 1982). The result was that a significant number of schools and adult centres in Great Britain used these behavioural practices.

A behaviourist view of teaching and learning means:

- *Curriculum design* was, and still is, heavily influenced by the Skills Analysis Model (Gardner et al., 1983) in which precise observable behaviours are sequentially arranged under discrete curricular headings. The model had a mechanistic quality which lies at the very core of behavioural theory ('if it moves- break it down!').

- *Assessment and recording* was structured to enable the teacher to track pupil progress through a pre-determined path of learning. Conciseness and precision became imperative. Qualitative comment was squeezed out in favour of the tick in the box or symbol to show the level of learning and generalisation of the skill.

- *Classroom organisation* and grouping of learners took on a character that enabled behavioural practice. At its simplest this resulted in individual instruction being seen as the only way of doing any serious or useful work with students with learning difficulties, a perspective which we would contend is still common. This was further reinforced by the assumption that such students are incapable of incidental learning, hence teaching must be externally controlled and precisely focused. Room management theory is a fine example of the result of imposing the structure perceived to be required by behavioural theory. Clearly defined roles for staff within the classroom are designed to maximise the efficiency and speed with which the student can progress through the extensively task- analysed learning material.

- *The language of special educational needs* contains certain phrases. Statements of special educational needs provide a good example of the way in which behavioural vocabulary dominates the language of SEN. Wording such as 'tasks must be broken down into small enough steps to enable the pupil to progress' is still common. It may well be that this is not consciously intended as a teaching advice but it nevertheless communicates an underlying belief in a set of teaching principles

---

By the mid-1980s an increasing uneasiness with behavioural practice was developing. Many teachers and other practitioners were feeling dissatisfaction with its mechanistic nature and with the fact that students taught this way did not seem able to transfer learning from one context to another. At the same time there is an acknowledgement that much has been learned from behaviourism, both in terms of its rigours and its theory. For example, teachers have become much more able to define their aims and objectives for students and to see the importance of precise recording and monitoring.

Interactive Approaches

It was at this point that interactive approaches to teaching started to awaken people's interest. These were *not* conceived as an alternative to behaviourism but as a framework that provided a wider picture of pupils' learning, solving some of the concerns of teachers.

Interactive approaches are derived from cognitive psychology and its interest in understanding the development of thinking. There is little to be gained in drawing sharp distinctions between behaviourism and cognitivism but placing the two approaches side-by-side provides teachers with a powerful set of tools for enabling learning. Indeed, this text assumes throughout that our encounters with behaviourism have provided us with a whole variety of (methodological) rigours and techniques that should be incorporated into all teaching practice.

The growth of interactive approaches in special education

- Interest in interactive approaches in the field of severe learning difficulties began to gather pace in the early 1980s following the two articles published in *Special Education* (now *The British Journal of Special Education*): McConkey, 1981; and Smith, Moore and Phillips, 1983. These writers questioned teachers' reliance on behavioural approaches as they felt that not enough attention was paid to enabling the development of students' understanding.

- During this time there was an increased interest in the educational implications of the work of the Soviet psychologist Vygotsky (Van Der Veer, 1991) and also in applying Piagetian theory of mental development to the difficulties experienced by children with impaired intellect.

- The importance of developing cognitive strategies to improve children's thinking also began to influence educationists, particularly Ashman and Conway (1989) in Australia and the Staff of Rectory Paddock School (1983) in England.

- A further influence at this time was the research into language carried out in Bristol by Gordon Wells (1986) and in London by Barbara Tizard and Martin Hughes (1984). These projects seemed to be revealing that young children with difficulties in learning benefit from an approach to teaching which draws on the principles of successful parent-child interactions.

- In the late 1980s there were two conferences in Birmingham. The first (Smith, 1987) sought to gather together like-minded individuals interested in the application of interactive approaches to teaching children with learning difficulties. The second (Smith, 1990) provided evidence of the compatibility of interactive approaches with the newly introduced National Curriculum. Work based, in particular, at Cambridge, Manchester and Birmingham Universities, continues the search for the most effective ways to encourage learning for those experiencing difficulties (Ashdown, Carpenter and Bovair 1991; Rose *et al.*, 1994; Sebba, Byers and Rose, 1993)

Interactive approaches, however, are not portrayed in this book as a series of *techniques* or as a *recipe* to be followed. Rather they are presented to readers as a series of *ideas* that are intended to cause them to question how they teach.

This is in contrast to the way in which behaviourism has been accessed to teachers. For example, the EDY course provides step-by-step training on techniques such as task analysis, shaping and imitation.

Where are we now?

At the time of writing (Spring, 1996), although schools are still struggling to make the National Curriculum work for pupils with learning difficulties, there is a breadth of approaches and a range of subjects which were not evident prior to 1988. The narrow, skills-based curriculum associated with special education has broadened enormously and teachers are anxious to harness the best both from this new freedom and from the old rigours of behaviourism. Many school curriculum documents are suffering a little from trying to maintain the best of both worlds. We hope that this book will help staff to use what they have learned to move their documents and, of course, their practice forward.

We also hope that this book will be of help to teachers of students with learning difficulties who do not work in schools. Community Care legislation has ensured that the majority of adults with learning disabilities can be found in small group homes, further and adult education colleges and social education centres. Life-long education is seen as important in all of these contexts and thus a variety of staff have taken on teaching roles. Many are struggling to find suitable approaches to encourage their clients or residents to continue to learn. A similar situation can be found in adult contexts as in schools. Behaviourism has had its hold but there is now beginning an interest in the relevance of interactive approaches. There is, of course, greater freedom for education in the adult world than in schools. National Curriculum and OFSTED have very specific demands during the school years which do not exist post-16 (or post-19 in some areas). It is hoped that staff who work with adults will find this book helpful as they develop ways in which they can teach and their clients can learn.

Is there a need for this text?

Obviously we think that there is! It is, however, important to establish whether there is a pre-existing requirement for in-service training in interactive approaches, or whether by writing this book we are merely generating the need. In order to test perceived needs of a representative group of teachers, Collis (1993) asked the following questions of 37 teachers of pupils with severe learning difficulties (using a two-stage questionnaire technique).

1. Is there a need for an INSET package that explores process rather than product based teaching?

There was a unanimous, 'Yes' response and a real interest expressed in exploring interactive approaches which were perceived as difficult to access and therefore implement. Also, there were feelings expressed that many teachers were in fact already teaching in an interactive manner. However, due to a lack of understanding of the underlying theoretical models, they found it difficult to develop further. There was a real need to clarify and pull together what is meant by interactive approaches and explore the implications for teachers.

2. What should the contents of such a package be?

The respondents indicated that they would like to see the following features within this type of INSET package:

- a theoretical underpinning;
- a balanced view of the approach, with an opportunity to explore both its advantages and disadvantages;
- clear description of methodology;
- the above delivered in an interactive manner.

With the development of locally managed schools with delegated budgets there has been a heightened impetus to ensure that INSET arranged by school managers is both efficient and effective. It must meet the needs of schools and individual teachers and give good value for money. Perhaps most importantly, it should be clearly linked to the development of the teaching and learning process. You may consider that to achieve all of this is a fairly tall order. However, it was partially with such school-based imperatives in mind that this package was designed.

Staff working in other settings have a very similar need for efficient and effective in-service education and this has further influenced the design of the course presented in this book.

Using this text

This text is designed to be used either as the basis of an in-service programme or simply to be read by individuals to enable them to explore interactive methods. We will elaborate on each of these.

... as an INSET package

The package is structured to form a programme of ten sessions intended to lead logically from one to the next. One possible model of delivery could be to run one session per week which could be fitted into an academic term within a school or college setting. Each session is planned to last between 1 and 2 hours, depending on how much reading is undertaken in advance. The text provides materials (for example OHP masters) that can be used at the discretion of the user.

It is hoped that some of those undertaking this in-service package may use it to contribute to gaining further professional qualification through such schemes as Accreditation of Prior Learning. Anyone who wishes to pursue this avenue should get in touch with their local Institute of Higher Education to discuss the matter

... as a textbook

The reader may simply treat the text as a means of becoming more familiar with interactive approaches. At the end of each session a list of further reading is intended to provide the most relevant texts relating to the subject matter. Throughout, however, it is hoped that the reader will take the opportunity to consider how what they read affects how they teach.

Each session is made up of four sections:

1. FOCUS

This consists of several pages of text which may be presented as an introduction to the topic, either by being read before, or at the beginning of the session. Alternatively this material may be used by a leader to support his or her presentation.

Material is presented in a way that is intended to be as accessible as possible. To achieve this, for example, the text contains few academic references. Instead the reader is provided with further and related reading at the end of each section, with notes relating to their particular relevance. Throughout, emphasis is placed on teasing out the practical relevance for the teacher.

2. REFLECTION

This consists of exercises and/or discussion points on which participants are asked to reflect and relate to their current practice. It refers directly to the focus for the session. Not surprisingly, the means of delivering this package is biased towards group interactive methods.

Participants are encouraged to debate how the focus material might influence their practice in the future.

3. HOW TO MOVE ON

This contains ideas of activities for the classroom and/or examples to illustrate the focus in action. (These may be contained within the text of the focus but debated at this point.)

4. ACTION PLAN

The way in which each participant responds to the ideas within the focus will be different. This section prompts participants into formulating how the issues discussed might have specific effects on their own practice and encourages them to make a plan of action which can be set in motion during the time following the session.

FEEDBACK

After the initial meeting each session will be preceded by an opportunity to feed back any ideas that have occurred to participants during the intervening period, and to report progress on action plans.

Throughout the text, it is our intention to make this in-service package interactive not only in its content but also in the means by which it encourages an understanding of this material. For example, readers are periodically challenged by questions designed to probe their understanding. These questions are those that occurred to us in the writing of the text and we have, therefore, usually provided our own responses.

Whether it is used as a training course or as a textbook, it is hoped that readers will find the ten sessions that follow this introduction useful in the development of their practice.

References

Ashdown, R., Carpenter, B. and Bovair, K. (1991) *The Curriculum Challenge: Access to the National Curriculum for Pupils with Learning Difficulties*. Lewes: Falmer Press.

Ashman, A. and Conway, R. (1989) *Cognitive Strategies for Special Education: Process Based Instruction*. London: Routledge.

Collis, M. (1993) *Research and Development into a Process Based INSET Package*. Unpublished MA Dissertation, University of London.

Foxen, T. and McBrien, J. (1981) *The EDY In-service Training Course for Mental Handicap Practitioners: Staff Training in Behavioural Methods*. Manchester: Manchester University Press.

Gardner, J., Murphy, J. and Crawford, N. (1983) *The Skills Analysis Model*. Kidderminster: BIMH.

McConkey, R. (1981) 'Education without understanding?', *Special Education*, **8** (3), 8-10.

Robson, C. (1982) *Language Development Through Structured Teaching*. Cardiff: Drake Educational Associates.

Rose, R., Fergusson, A., Coles, C., Byers, R. and Banes, D. (1994) *Implementing the Whole Curriculum for Pupils with Learning Difficulties*. London: David Fulton Publishers.

Sebba, J., Byers, R. and Rose, R. (1993) *Redefining the Whole Curriculum for Pupils with Learning Difficulties*. London: David Fulton Publishers.

Smith, B. (1989) 'Which Approach? The Education of Children with Severe Learning Difficulties', *Mental Handicap*, **17** (3), 111-14.

Smith, B. Moore, Y. and Phillips, C (1983) 'Education with Understanding?' *Special Education*, **10** (2), 21-24.

Smith, B. (1987) *Interactive Approaches to the Education of Children with Severe Learning Difficulties*. Birmingham: Westhill College.

Smith, B. (1990*) Interactive Approaches to Teaching the Core Subjects*. Bristol: Lame Duck Publishing.

Staff of Rectory Paddock School (1983) *In Search of a Curriculum* (2nd edn.) Sidcup: Robin Wren Publications.

Tizard, B. and Hughes, M. (1984) *Young Children Learning*. London: Fontana.

Van Der Veer, R. (1991) *Understanding Vygotsky*. Oxford: Blackwell.

Wells, G. (1986) *The Meaning Makers*. London: Hodder and Stoughton.

SESSION 1

What are Interactive Approaches?

In this session we provide a background to interactive approaches by describing some of the differing ways in which this term has been interpreted, offering the reader some reasons for the development of this way of working and attempting to show why it is needed.

This focus differs from all others in that it is all about providing a theoretical background and therefore necessarily includes a considerable number of references. We have divided these into recommended further reading and a more formal reference section.

1. Focus

Definition

There is no one definition of interactive approaches to the teaching of students with learning difficulties. It is, however, possible to tease out some of the central themes. Figure 1.1 is an attempt to present the different aspects visually.

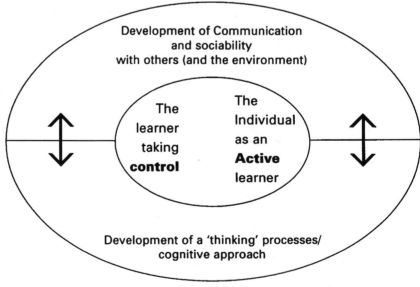

Figure 1.1

The central circle describes the fundamentals of interactive approaches whilst the outer circle illustrates the two main themes that have resulted.

Active learners

Central to all definitions of interactive approaches is that *learners are active modifiers of the information they receive*. They do not simply sit and soak up information but learn most efficiently when they are actively involved. In most cases this will mean engaging with other people but it can also mean actively engaging with things. It is vital that *the learner's brain is actively engaged in a given task*. It is very easy to be convinced that students are learning actively when they have table-top activities in front of them. But is this really engaging their brains?

Taking Control

How then can we ensure that the learner is active? Smith (1994) suggests that an overall aim should be to enable learners 'to have an effect on the operation and outcomes' of their own lives. This is conceived of as a process of *taking control* and can range in practice from choosing which toy to play with to making major decisions concerning job opportunities.

For some students with learning difficulties taking full control over their lives may be impracticable, in which case it may be more realistic to aim for them to 'have an effect' on the operation and outcomes of their lives.

Traditional teaching approaches can sometimes have the opposite effect. Rather than enabling students to become independent thinkers, they produce within them a state of 'learned helplessness' (Seligman, 1975), in which they have learned to be more dependent upon adults than they really need to be. Students have been taught a multitude of isolated skills without the development of those thought processes which would enable them to use these effectively and when needed.

Consequences for Teaching

We must be quite clear about the overall aims we have for the students we teach. If we are indeed keen to enable them to be active learners and to have an effect on the operation and outcomes within their lives, this will directly affect the style of teaching that we adopt.

Interactive approaches can encourage students to show self-regulatory behaviour through enabling them to confront problems themselves with understanding and active decision making. Teachers need to begin by providing much of the regulation but their aim is to pass this over to students so that they are eventually taking control themselves. The teacher's style and role becomes one of enabling students to become active in their own learning.

The notion of enabling learners to take control is clearly linked with encouraging them to take responsibility. This suggests that if control is offered, they develop a sense of responsibility, in a general sense, for their own learning and start to understand why they should learn.

From this central principle we will identify two distinct, yet complementary themes, which are represented by the two halves of the outer circle in Figure 1.1.

1. The Importance of Communication

> Human development is fundamentally a joint enterprise between child and caregiver. Cognitive functions require a social context for their initial emergence and subsequent facilitation before they eventually become internalised as properties of the individual.
>
> (Schaffer, 1977)

For those working with students at the early stages of development whatever their chronological age, an important theoretical underpinning for interactive approaches has been found in the development of communication in the first year of life of a normally developing infant. The approach stems from a study of interactions between mother and infant, which reveals aspects that can then be adopted by teachers. For example, Christie *et al.* (1992) looked at the development of rapport between mother and child as a means of identifying an effective vehicle for learning. He drew attention to the process of imitation between mother and child which leads to learning through a pattern of interactions.

One of the most recent and clear extensions of this line of thought is that described in intensive interaction developed by Nind and Hewett (1994). This very practically based approach is centred on the development of sociability and is particularly relevant to those with severe and profound learning difficulties. Their assumption is that the ability to be social is the precursor to communication. The approach is grounded in the development of sociability, through 'mutually satisfying interactions'. From this, springs a whole methodology, which in their words is 'less about formal teaching or training and more about facilitating learning'.

2. The Importance of Thinking Processes

Bruner (1977) argues that there are strong links between growth in the ability to communicate and the development of thinking. We have tried to represent this in Figure 1.1 with the double arrows which represent the interlinking of the two elements the outer circle.

Several educationists have developed approaches that value the development of mental structures (e.g. the ability to solve problems), that will thereby enable the student to take control. Theoretical background can in particular be drawn from the work of Vygotsky and Flavell. Vygotsky's (1978) work highlighted the notion of mental development being dependent on social interaction during problem solving and practical activity. Flavell also has this emphasis:

> For the majority of people, I suspect other human beings and their activities constitute the most interesting and challenging objects of thought that their daily lives afford and much of their richest and most complex cognitions may be social interactions.
>
> (Flavell, 1977)

Based on such premises, the development of the student as an increasingly independent problem solver becomes the aim.

Teaching becomes not only a process of ensuring that students possess a range of possible responses to a given practical problem, but also that they are aware of this repertoire and the need for its flexible use. They must come to understand which learned strategy is appropriate to which situation.

It is at this point that *metacognition* can be introduced as a means of developing a greater consciousness of the variety of ways of achieving goals, through effective problem solving. Metacognition may best be conceptualised as 'thinking about thinking', and simplistically represented in the Figure 1.2. Students' abilities to solve problems are dependent on their degree of awareness of and hence the ability to have control over what they are thinking.

A. Simple Metacognition
'John was thinking about Mary'
If a student hears this sentence, s/he will require metacognitive ability to understand it.

B. More difficult
'John was thinking about Mary who was thinking about Fred'
This involves quite sophisticated understanding of 'thinking about thinking'.

Figure 1.2

Ashman and Conway's Process Based Instruction (1989, 1993) provides a good example of a methodology arising from such a thinking skills approach. Their detailed account describes the process of encouraging the learner to form 'plans' as a means of solving problems. A plan is a mental image of how to solve a problem, represented in the form of sequence of activities or thoughts and is further explored in Session 4 'Problem Solving'.

In summary the most important aspects of interactive approaches are drawn together following four interdependent features.

The learner must:

• *take control*
• *be active*
• *develop communication and sociability*
• *develop thinking processes.*

What have been the Problems with Traditional Approaches?

It is important to engage in a realistic discussion about those aspects of traditional approaches which lead us to look elsewhere for guidance. We should not do this in a purely negative way, for an examination of existing approaches may equally lead to identification of positives that we should retain within our battery of techniques. It is vital, however, that we satisfy ourselves that we are not simply dismissing 'old' approaches in favour of the next fashion in teaching approaches.

Table 1.1 summarises some of the main concerns that have been raised.

Table 1.1 What have people found to be some of the problems in using purely a behavioural style?

A. Concerns resulting from the nature of behaviourism:

- Its reductionist nature leads to:
  - over-simplification (Bray *et al.*, 1988)
  - problems with generalisation (Sugden, 1989)
  - learning without understanding (Farrell, 1991)
- It emphasises what is taught rather than what is learnt (Billinge, 1988)
- It is concerned only with the 'observable' (Sugden, 1989)
- It casts the learner into a passive role (Jordan and Powell, 1991)
- It is commonly used without sufficient emphasis on generalisation

B. Concerns resulting from its usage:

- It has proven open to abuse, for example, in its usage to teach all subjects (Hewett and Nind, 1989)
- Emphasises the importance of the product of learning rather than the process itself (Smith *et al.*, 1983)
- It forms the rhetoric rather than the practice of special education (Jordan and Powell, 1991)
- The teacher is seen as a technician rather than educator (Guess, Benson and Seigel-Causey, 1985)
- It is teacher led, leading to learned helplessness in the student (Seligman 1975)

Behavioural competence provides a cloak of competence, afforded by being able to perform certain activities without help

(Wood and Shears, 1986)

It does not enable people to take significant decisions about their life circumstances and directly participate in controlling their own lives

(Smith, 1994)

It is not our intention to focus in detail on these concerns though we, and many other practitioners, have been left feeling that there must be more to teaching than this.

So where do we go from here? What is the place of a behavioural style of teaching? How can we make use of and exploit our experiences of a behavioural style?

What have we learnt from using behaviourism as a theoretical background?

- the importance of a systematic approach
- the importance of gathering evidence of learning
- the importance of clarity and precision
- the importance of clear identification of roles
- the importance of setting conditions: behaviour does not occur in isolation
- the importance of baseline measurement
- the introduction of specific techniques to promote the development of skills (e.g. prompting/ task analysis/ reinforcement/ fading)

What are the contexts in which such an approach may be useful?

- The development of some self-help skills for example:
  - either (i) when it is important that the learner simply learns the skill with understanding as being of secondary importance (e.g. should not open the medicine cabinet – for some learners the priority may simply be that they don't try the pills and understanding why not is of secondary importance;
  - or (ii) when the skill is conducive to being broken down into a sequence of steps, although it may not be enough to teach without understanding (e.g. teeth cleaning, shoelace tying).
- Development of rote counting skills, as a precursor to a fuller understanding of numbers.
- Development of some types of knowledge (e.g. address, birthday, dates, rivers).
- Development of a new skill before it can be put into practice (e.g. crossing a road in the playground before crossing a real road).

In summary, a behavioural style may be extremely useful when there is no immediate need for understanding. Perhaps, for example, a detailed understanding may even hamper the reflexive use of a skill, and understanding may indeed follow at higher levels of development.

This is necessarily a very brief and limited account. The two critiques of Smith (1983) and Farrell (1991) form a very interesting comparison of views.

How can an Interactive Approach Resolve these Concerns?

In this first session we have attempted to sum up some of the central principles of interactive approaches in preparation for considering certain aspects in more detail in subsequent sessions. It is hoped that teachers will engage with the text to question their own principles and thus develop their practice.

The principles of an interactive approach

- Learning is contingent upon good interpersonal relationships.
- There is sensitivity to feedback from the learner.
- Focus is on understanding rather than skill acquisition.
- Emphasis is on respect, negotiation and participation (positive regard). The student's contribution is valued and positively built upon. (Nind and Hewett's approach is a good example of the value placed on respect for the learner.)
- It is a process based approach, in which the quality of teaching and learning is as important as the performance of the objectives – the quality of the process becomes the objective. The teacher should therefore have a clear understanding of the process to be undertaken rather than the end to be reached.
- Teaching is not always dependent on dividing that which is to be taught into its constituent parts.
- It is based on intrinsic motivation, rather than on extrinsic reward (the student doesn't have to be bribed).
- It is not the learner who fails to learn but the teacher who fails to provide an adequate learning opportunity.

> **Some of the more common features 9f interactive approaches**
> - Positive cycles of success breeding success.
> - Use of games and everyday routines.
> - Importance of naturalistic observations.
> - Adult follows or capitalises on the initiations of the learner.
> - Learner plays an active role in the choice of what is to be learned.
> - Dialogue between less experienced and more experienced.
> - Allows for learning through mistakes, within a safe environment.
> - Leads to social and emotional maturity, through the development of independent learning and personal autonomy.
> - Learning takes place in meaningful contexts.

2. Reflection

In groups of about four:

1. Discuss concrete examples from your own practice of using:
   (a) an interactive approach
   (b) a behavioural approach.

2. Taking just one of these examples for each member of the group ask yourselves the following questions:
   (a) What did the student/s do?
   (b) What did they learn?
   (c) How worthwhile was it?
   (d) What did I do?
   (e) What did I learn?
   (f) What am I going to do next?

(From Ashton *et al.*, 1980)

3. Moving On

Using a routine teaching activity (for example you might choose 'drinks time') carefully list the opportunities to fulfil the four central themes of interactive approaches:

- Taking control.
- Active learning.
- Communication and sociability.
- Thinking processes.

4. Action Plan

Plan one activity during the course of your week with these four principles in mind. Carry out this plan and be prepared to discuss what happened at the , beginning of the next session. (NB. You may wish to consider using video tape.)

Further Reading	Reference	Points of Interest
	Ashman, A. and Conway, R. (1993) *Using Cognitive Methods in the Classroom.* London: Routledge.	Importance of thinking/ problem solving.
	Coupe J., O'Kane, J. and Smith, B. (1994) *Taking Control: Enabling People with Learning Difficulties.* London: David Fulton Publishers	Student as active learner.
	Farrell, P. (1991) 'Behavioural and interactive teaching for children with severe learning difficulties: : Match or mismatch?', *Educational and Child Psychology,* 8(2), 61–68.	The place of behaviourism.
	McGee, J., Melnolascino, F., Hobbs, D. and Menousek, P. (1987) *Gentle Teaching: A Non-aversive Approach to Helping Persons with Mental Retardation.* New York: Human Sciences Press.	Respect for the learner.
	Nind, M. and Hewett, D. (1994) *Access to Communication: Developing the Basics of Communication with People with Severe Learning Difficulties through Intensive Interaction.* London: David Fulton Publishers	Importance of communication and social interaction.

References

Ashman, A. and Conway, C. (1989) *Cognitive Strategies for Special Education: Process Based Instruction.* London: Routledge.

Ashman, A. and Conway, R. (1993) *Using Cognitive Methods in the Classroom.* London: Routledge.

Ashton, P,. Hunt, P., Jones, S. and Watson, G. (1980) *Curriculum in Action: An Approach to Evaluation.* Milton Keynes: Open University Press.

Billinge, R. (1988) 'The objectives model of curriculum development: a creaking bandwagon', *Mental Handicap,* 16(1), 26–29.

Bray, A., MacArthur, J. and Ballard, K. (1988) 'Education of pupils with profound learning disabilities: Issues of policy, curriculum, teaching methods and evaluation', *European Journal of Special Needs Education,* 3(4), 207-224.

Bruner, J. (1977) 'Early social Interaction and language acquisition'. In Shaffer, H. (ed.) *Studies in Mother-Infant Interaction.* New York: Academic Press.

Christie, P., Newson, E., Newson, J. and Prevezer,W. (1992) 'An interactive approach to language and communication for non speaking children'. In Lane, D. and Miller, A. (eds) *Child and Adolescent Therapy: A Handbook.* Milton Keynes: Open University Press.

Farrell, P. (1991) 'Behavioural and interactive teaching for children with severe learning difficulties: match or mismatch?' *Educational and Child Psychology,* 8(2), 61-68.

Flavell, J. (1977) *Cognitive Development.* London: Prentice-Hall.

Guess, D., Benson, H. and Seigal-Causey, E. (1985) 'Concepts and issues related to choice making and autonomy among persons with severe disabilities', *Journal of the Association of Persons with Severe Handicaps,* 10(2), 79-86.

Hewett, D. and Nind, M. (1989) 'Developing an interactive curriculum for pupils with severe and complex learning difficulties. A classroom process'. In Smith, B. (ed.) *Interactive Approaches to the Education of Children with Severe Learning Difficulties.* Birmingham: Westhill College.

Jordan, R. and Powell, S. (1991) 'Teaching thinking: the case for principles ', *European Journal of Special Needs Education,* 6(2), 112-123.

Nind, M. and Hewett, D. (1994) *Access to Communication: Developing the Basics of Communication with People with Severe Learning Difficulties through Intensive Interaction.* London: David Fulton Publishers.

Robson, W. (1989) 'Teaching effective thinking', *Special Children,* 29, 20-22.

Schaffer, H. (1977) 'Early interactive development'. In Shaffer, H. (ed.) *Studies in Mother -infant Interaction.* London:Academic Press.

Seligman, M. (1975) *Helplessness: On Depression Development and Death* San Francisco: Freeman

Smith, B. (ed.) (1987) *Interactive Approaches to the Education of Children with Severe Learning Difficulties.* Birmingham: Westhill College.

Smith, B. (1989) 'Which approach? The education of pupils with severe learning difficulties', *Mental Handicap,* 17(3), 111-114.

Smith, B. (1994) 'Handing over control to people with learning difficulties.' In Coupe- O'Kane, J. and Smith, B. (eds) *Taking Control: Enabling People with Learning Difficulties.* London: David Fulton Publishers.

Smith, B., Moore, Y. and Phillips, C.J. (1983) 'Education with understanding?', *Special Education: Forward Trends,* 10(2), 21–24.

Sugden, D. (1989) Cognitive *Approaches in Special Education.* Lewes: Falmer Press.

Vygotsky, L. (1978) *Mind in Society: The Development of Higher Psychological Processes.* Cambridge: Harvard University Press.

Wood, S. and Shears, B. (1986) *Teaching Children with Severe Learning Difficulties: A Radical Reappraisal.* Beckenham: Croom Helm.

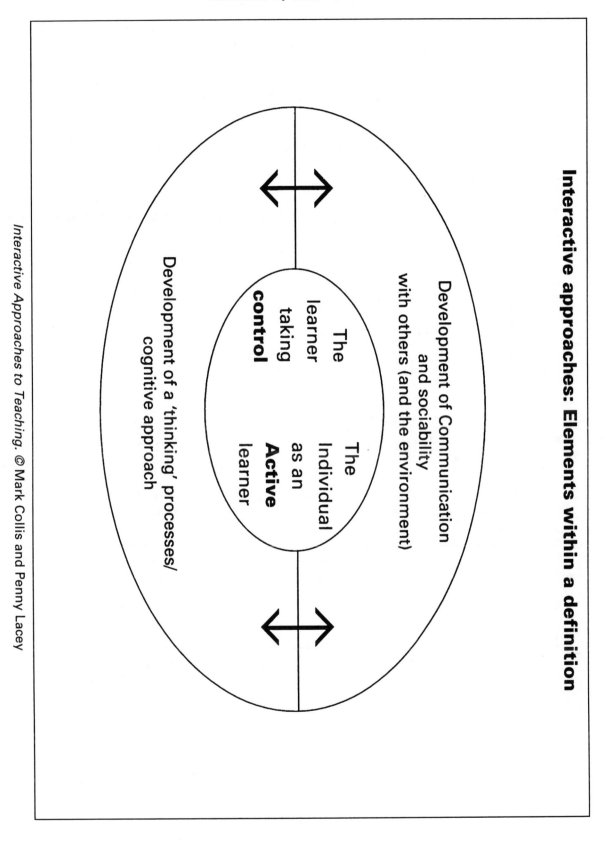

Interactive approaches: Elements within a definition

Development of Communication
and sociability
with others (and the environment)

The
learner
taking
control

The
Individual
as an
Active
learner

Development of a 'thinking' processes/
cognitive approach

The principles of an interactive approach

- Learning is contingent upon good interpersonal relationships

- There is sensitivity to feedback from the learner.

- Focus is on understanding rather than skill acquisition.

- Emphasis is on respect, negotiation and participation (positive regard). The student's contribution is valued and positively built upon.

- It is a process based approach, in which the quality of teaching and learning is as important as the performance of the objectives – the quality of the process becomes the objective. The teacher should therefore have a clear understanding of the process to be undertaken rather than the end to be reached.

- Teaching is not always dependent on dividing that which is to be taught into its constituent parts.

- It is based on intrinsic motivation, rather than on extrinsic reward (the student doesn't have to be bribed).

- It is not the learner who fails to learn but the teacher who fails to provide an adequate learning opportunity

Interactive Approaches to Teaching. © Mark Collis and Penny Lacey

SESSION 2

Interactive Teaching Methods

The teaching approaches which form the bedrock of working in an interactive manner are explored in this second session. Aspects chosen for discussion include: games, interactive routines, open-ended activities, natural situations, topics and the importance of enabling students to gain some control over their learning.

1. Focus

At their simplest, interactive teaching approaches are those in which learners are encouraged to interact with their environment in a manner which would suggest that the activities are rewarding in themselves. Learners are encouraged to be active in their responses. This does not necessarily mean that they have to move around or do something outward. The action can be entirely in the mind. It is, however, never a passive response. It will always engage the intellect, the imagination or the emotions of the learner.

One of the most important ingredients of interactive activities is that they are fun, whether that fun is very energetic or quiet and tranquil. Problems with motivation dissolve if teachers engage learners in doing things that are genuinely enjoyable. Some learners with the most profound learning difficulties challenge their teachers considerably in terms of motivation but the use of very detailed observation can usually reveal that some indications of pleasure and rejection which can be built upon whilst engaging in playful activities. A published tool which is very useful for this is the Affective Communication Assessment. This was developed by Coupe et al. (1985) specifically for students at a very early stage of development.

Games

Games are very important at all stages of the lives of human beings. They can certainly be motivating if they are matched exactly to the needs of the player. Not everyone likes the same games and no one enjoys a game which is too easy or too difficult. But when the context, the content, the intensity of involvement and the level of difficulty are right most people are easily engaged and respond very positively.

Games are all essentially playful but there is an enormous range of activities, from peek-a-boo to chess, which can be classified under the generic title. Some activities are almost completely unstructured whilst others are highly complicated and contain complex rules and regulations. At whatever level, there is enormous potential for learning within games. *Essentially they provide a model for the learner to follow and that model is repeated again and again.* An experienced player provides this model and can support the learner through pointing out errors and encouraging repeated trials. Also, as it is only a game, mistakes are acceptable and it is safe to practise. It is important for learners to feel secure both physically and emotionally if they are to progress in their learning. Games provide both safety and security in a highly predictable manner.

For those learners who are at the earliest stages of development, much can be made of games which might be associated with mothers and young babies. These contain the elements of imitation, gently dramatised behaviour, rhythm, bursts and pauses in the activity, simplified and exaggerated language and they may be physical in nature. Outcomes are usually unknown at the start and the mother enters the world of the child rather than expecting the infant to understand her world. The best mother-infant games are relaxed and joyful and give plenty of opportunities for the child to take the lead in terms of content and pace.

Many teachers of learners who are at this early stage of development but who are chronologically older, might argue that it is not age appropriate to play infant games with them. But it is also possible to argue that there is much to be learned from these playful situations that make them an invaluable tool in the armoury of their teachers. Age appropriateness need not be a problem if it is more related to respect for individuals and enabling them to take some control over their own lives than to whether teenagers and adults should indulge in childish activities. This is not an easy dilemma to resolve and further reading on the subject is recommended, e.g. Nind and Hewett (1994).

The example which follows contains an interactive game suitable for a learner at the earliest stages of development. It has been taken from the work of Nind and Hewett and can be found in the book cited above.

> Colin has profound visual and hearing impairments. He has been socially remote for nearly all of his life, preferring his own world of rhythmic movements and noises. For him, interactions involving exchanges of behaviour means romping and rolling on a crash mat, hugging, pulling and especially spending long periods with faces pressed together.
>
> (Nind and Hewett, 1994, p.132)

We have included in the appendix a chapter by Dave Hewett, entitled *How To Start Doing Intensive Interaction.* It is particularly helpful for teachers working with the most profoundly disabled students but it is hoped that it will be of interest to all readers.

For learners who are more advanced in their development, the principles behind intensive interaction can be incorporated into more complex interactive games. These can range from simple turn-taking and cause and effect routines to traditional card and board games. Devising games for developing mathematical understanding is part of the training video presented by Roy

McConkey, called *Count Me In* (McConkey and McEvoy, 1986). This was made for parents and teachers and contains many ideas for home-made games which use a small number of concepts at any one time. One game involves the use of a home-made die on which four sides have the same number and two sides are blank. Players take it in turns to throw the die and count out objects to match their throw. There are lots of opportunities for counting the same number and the presence of blanks makes it possible to have a winner.

The challenge for the teacher is to design the game so that it incorporates the learning intended but at the same time enables learners to pursue aspects that interest them. This involves detailed knowledge of the level of ability of each of the learners and their preferred learning styles as well as an imaginative approach to devising games.

> A group of teenagers with learning difficulties had been working on improving the way they listen to each other in group situations. The teacher devised a series of music and drama games to support their discussions. The first was a nonsense conversation between two students using 'ooh, ah and oh' instead of words. Attention was drawn to tone of voice and inflexion to get meaning across. A variation on this game was one where partners used each other's names but no other words. Another related game involved using a musical instrument to denote the speaker in a conversation. This was passed between the two 'speakers' who used it to 'say' something. As there was only one instrument only one person could 'speak' at once thus giving practice at listening and waiting turns. The significance of the games were pointed out to the students to reinforce the learning.

Interactive Routines

From the work of researchers such as Wells (1986), it is possible to understand the importance of simple interactive routines for the development of communication and spoken language. Wells suggests that the most effective way in which teachers encourage learners to develop effective language skills is to embed talk in the natural routines in which the learners are involved. Young children are constantly involved in washing, eating, dressing, going to the shops etc. and they build up understanding of the routines and the language (scripts) attached to them as they repeat them day after day. Parents provide running commentaries and endless repetitions of vocabulary from which their children learn.

> The potential for learning in joint action routines (Snyder-McLean *et al.*, 1984) between a learner and an adult can be summed up in the following ways:
> - they require the learner to be active;
> - they provide experience of the dynamic and reciprocal nature of communication;
> - sessions are structured without appearing to be so;
> - the planning scheme is content free so it can be adapted to learners of different ages and with varying abilities and interests;
> - the structure of the routine provides a 'scaffold' so it is easier for learner to respond appropriately.

A simple example of an early joint action routine is a co-operative turn-taking game such as rolling a ball between partners. 'Ready, steady, go' may be appropriate or eye contact might be the only means of communication but the routine is simple and repetitive.

The daily round people with learning difficulties is full of natural possibilities for developing interactive routines from arriving at school or the centre, through drinking, eating and visiting the bathroom; to getting ready to return home. Many other activities are also repeated constantly, such as getting out equipment and returning it, getting ready for swimming or a shopping trip, moving from room to room or greeting and saying goodbye to people. These are often the times of the day that are considered to be breaks between teaching times but in fact they are moments that have enormous potential for learning communication and social skills, especially if teachers actively seize the opportunities and structure them to provide practice at different scripts.

At a more basic level, work with profoundly disabled students involves building up the routines in short simple bursts, using cues to enable anticipation within the routine. For example the toileting routine could begin with the presentation of a piece of nappy or a miniature potty or a chain handle, depending upon the level of understanding and level of toilet ability of the student. This signals the beginning of the routine which should then always be carried out in the same way. Simple language can be used to accompany the activity such as 'stand up' 'hold on' or 'legs up'. It is useful to choose language which will be repeated many times during each routine. Anticipation can be encouraged through pausing and expecting active involvement even if the student is not able to move independently.

For more able students, routines can still offer opportunities for language and cognitive development, particularly if the routine is changed in some way as this encourages problem solving. It may, for instance, be usual to place all the chairs in a semi-circle for discussion time. On some occasions there deliberately may not be enough chairs for everyone or the space that is usually used has been filled with boxes or all the chairs have been taken outside. This will create a situation that will involve some thought, alternative strategies and, with judicial questioning from staff, appropriate language.

Generally, using sabotage to change known situations or established routines into a problem solving exercise is a very helpful teaching approach. It generates extensive opportunities for focused learning if used systematically in a planned way. Like the games described earlier, it gives rise to practising thinking skills in a safe environment which is essentially playful and students become very involved in finding the latest thing that you have changed to provide them with 'food for thought'. Of course problem solving can be introduced in other ways, and Session 4 contains more about this.

Open-ended activities

Behavioural approaches demand specificity for activities. Exactly what should happen has been decided in advance. Interactive approaches are more open-ended and encourage both learner and teacher to be open-minded concerning what might happen, what should be the outcome and ultimately what should be learned, although this does not mean that the teacher cannot predict what might be learned from an activity. Much use is made of experiential activities where equipment is provided and different things are tried out. The teacher may be experimenting alongside the learner which can have the effect of encouraging the imitation. New ideas can be introduced this way, though they must match closely to the abilities of the student or they will probably be ignored or produce frustration.

For almost guaranteed interest and learning potential, open-ended activities should be developed from the initiations of the student. You know yourself how much easier it is to learn something in which you are interested and actively want to learn. Wells' research (1986) demonstrated this very clearly with the early language learning of young children. Those children whose parents followed their lead in conversations were seen to make the greatest progress in language learning. Wells suggests that we should try to recreate this situation in educational establishments, encouraging staff to listen attentively and take up the interests of the students rather than expect them to be interested in subjects arbitrarily chosen for them.

Natural Situations

Although there may be some occasions when learning should be taken out of context, generally learning is best embedded in natural situations. Dressing and undressing are more effectively learned if they are attached to real need, for example for swimming or gymnastics. For older students still needing practice in dressing, spending half a term on a daily keep-fit programme can improve both the dressing and the fitness. It can also be a good opportunity to improve counting, directional vocabulary, imitation and sequencing skills.

Observation and assessment using natural situations give a very good baseline from which to work with students with learning difficulties. The teacher can assess counting ability through providing opportunities for laying the table or finding out how many seats there are on the bus before deciding who should go on a shopping trip. Real-life situations can reveal much about the actual understanding of the individual which can contribute to any classroom activities observed.

Making use of natural situations is not a matter of stepping aside and waiting for the moment to arise. There was a popular misconception of the work of Piaget which encouraged many teachers to believe in waiting for 'reading readiness' or 'writing readiness' in young children. It is impossible to get children to learn things which are a long way from their present attainment but it is certainly possible to provide opportunities and encouragement for the next steps. Good interactive teachers create natural situations which provide the support necessary for incremental development. For instance, handling of coins may be an important next stage for a group of students. Buying at the shops may not be a daily possibility but creating a situation in school or centre where money can change hands several times a day will accelerate learning. Money can be recyclable and used for 'buying' lunch, drinks, books and pens or for providing services. The students know what they are practising and why and although it is contrived the context is natural.

Using natural contexts is also about not missing an opportunity for learning to take place. Moving around the school or centre can include directions, simple maps, locational vocabulary, memory garnes and much more. A jacuzzi session can mean exercises, singing, dressing, communication, anticipation, expressing likes and dislikes as well as water play. No activity is too mundane to be utilised.

Integrated Learning and Topics

There are many possibilities for planning opportunities for using games and routines in the curriculum so that students can practise skills intensively in natural contexts. Many schools and centres use a topic or integrated approach, finding that the active methods and unification of traditional subjects give students plenty of opportunities to practise the same skills and processes in many different ways. This helps to prevent boredom for both students and teachers, especially when many years are needed before something is learned.

For older students a broad-based topic in which to embed routines can be useful, especially if it has an 'ordinary life' perspective. Gardening or woodwork or household skills are particularly appropriate for integrating all kinds of learning. For instance, young adults who need to perfect their bed-making skills could offer a service to the local community for a 6-week period. This could include studying maps of the local area, following directions and practising road sense, time keeping, simple book-keeping and planning, as well as the bedmaking which is the excuse for the topic. Other services could follow this so that some of the skills built up can be utilised in slightly different contexts. Younger students can also make use of integrated learning situations, especially in the topics usually associated with primary practice, such as 'Transport' or 'Myself'. Routines are inherent in 'looking after myself' (teeth cleaning, washing, hairbrushing) and games can be invented using vehicle vocabulary and to enable students to begin to understand the science of movement (racing toy cars down a ramp).

There is more on topic work in Session 9 Curriculum Design.

Handing over Control

The ultimate aim of interactive teaching approaches is to enable students to be as independent as possible, to have an effect on their own lives and be able to make their own decisions. It is too late to wait until children reach secondary school age or adulthood to introduce responsibility and decision making. It must begin as early as possible. A popular way to begin this process is to encourage choice in food and drink. It is also frequently cited as the only way in which responsibility is handed over. Interactive teaching approaches treat this as the beginning only. Teachers want their students to take the lead in their own learning. They become experienced in observing students and knowing when to intervene and when to stand back. They know when to encourage negotiation concerning what should be learned. They are also skilled at providing natural contexts in which learning can be embedded. It is a sensitive job which, at times, is risky. How can you be sure about what is being learned? Careful observation will probably reveal learning that you had not thought off but then, that is very exciting.

Teaching in an interactive manner challenges teachers' attitudes and values. Traditionally teachers are in control: they know what they are going to teach. They decide when learning will take place, what the activities will be and what has been learned. Passing over control assumes a change in attitude. This can be uncomfortable, particularly for teachers who have spent many years developing their behavioural techniques. Like all change, it is best for it to happen gradually, building on what has gone before.

2. *Reflection*

This activity is similar to that in the previous session but more detail is needed to enable you to consider your own teaching approaches in depth.

With a partner or in a small group, brainstorm the different teaching approaches you use. Justify to yourselves why you are teaching in these ways. List them all but circle or star those which you feel fall under the label 'interactive approaches'. Take one of these and list at least four examples of its use.

This exercise is meant to provide an opportunity to discuss the ideas presented in the focus so be sure to spend adequate time airing your views.

3. *How to move on*

Using your partner or group for sounding out ideas, plan a half-term topic or module of work which integrates several aspects of the work to be covered by your students. In the planning, concentrate on the following features of interactive teaching and learning:

1. Social interaction.
2. Games.
3. Sabotage.
4. Problem solving.
5. Interactive daily routines.
6. Open-ended and experiential activities.
7. Natural contexts.
8. Handling over control to students.

4. *Action plan*

Take the activity you would like to do first in this topic/ module and plan it in more detail so that it is ready to try during the time between this session and the next. You may like to use the six questions quoted in the first session to help you to evaluate:

1. What did the students actually do?
2. What did they learn?
3. How worthwhile was it?
4. What did I do?
5. What did I learn?
6. What do I intend to do next?

You could use this half-term plan as the basis for development during this course, refining and improving it as you move through the sessions.

Further Reading	*Reference*	*Points of Interest*
	Coupe, J., Barton, L., Barber, M., Collins, L., Levy, D. and Murphy, D. (1985) *Affective Communication Assessment.* Manchester: MEC. Available from Melland School, Holmcroft Road, Manchester M19 7NG	Assessment of learners at an early stage of development.
	McConkey, R. and McEvoy, J. (1986) *Count Me In.* Dublin: St Michael's House.	Video course on devising simple number games for use with students with a variety of abilities and ages.
	Nind, M. and Hewett, D. (1994) *Access to Communication.* London: David Fulton Publishers.	The theoretical background to and the practicalities of intensive interaction.
	Snyder-McClean, L., Solomonson, B., McClean, J. and Sack, S. (1984) 'Structuring joint action routines: a strategy for facilitating communication and language development in the classroom', *Seminars in Speech and Language,* 5(3), 213-225.	Theoretical background and the practicalities of structuring joint action routines.
	Wells, G. (1986) *The Meaning Makers.* Oxford: Blackwell.	An account of the Bristol research into the way in which young children develop spoken language and what this means for teachers in schools.

Features of Interactive Approaches to Teaching and Learning

1. Social interaction

2. Games

3. Sabotage

4. Problem solving

5. Interactive daily routines

6. Open-ended and experiential activities

7. Natural contexts

8. Handing over control to students

Interactive Approaches to Teaching. © Mark Collis and Penny Lacey

SESSION 3

The Role of Teacher and Learner

The aim of this session is firstly to contrast the traditional role of the teacher–learner relationship with that of an interactive approach and secondly to explore the different facets of that interactive teaching role.

1. Focus

The following tables are designed to provide a stark insight into the difference in role between a traditional teacher perspective and that of the interactive approach. Of course this provides descriptions of the extremes and in real life most of us will be working somewhere on the continuum between the two positions.

Table 3.2 Model One: The traditional role within the teaching process

Issue	Teacher's role	Student's role
Information is conveyed in one direction	Imparter of knowledge – providing the learner with a set of directions	Receiver of information
Control over learning process	In control of the path of learning	Student follows lead
Context of learning	Controller of the environment	Passive recipient

Within this model teachers are seen as *trainers*. It is their responsibility to determine *what, how, when, and if* learning takes place. Students become the (passive) recipients of information deemed to be what they need. There is no dialogue or consultation about the content or method of teaching. The teacher proceeds in a mechanical way to deliver the material, potentially in the same way irrespective of the needs of the learner. The nature of the delivery changes according to the task rather than according to the learner. The focus is on what is taught, analysing a task down to its sub-steps. This argument should be qualified by saying that this can be, but by no means has to be the case. Behavioural techniques can be used in a way that results in involving learners in decision making about what and how they learn.

The description of the role so far may convey a negative feeling. However it may be the most effective and appropriate in a variety of teaching situations. As might be expected when the learner needs simply to perform a certain skill this may be achieved most thoroughly and rapidly by limiting the dialogue between the parties. This level of urgency may be necessary for example when teaching survival skills.

This leads on to another significant issue which is that of *power*, and where this resides within the relationship. As teachers or teaching figures most of us have been inculcated with the importance of maintaining control and authority within the group, or over the group. It appears to be tied up with issues of teacher credibility. Power must reside with the teacher for learning to take place. Model Two (below) questions aspects of this assumption, suggesting that classroom discipline can co-exist with negotiated learning.

Ask yourself:
- Why do I need to exert the amount of control of learning that I do?
- What are the circumstances in which I need to adopt a traditional role?
- Are there certain groups of students who respond well to a traditional approach?
- Is this the most effective style of teaching, to achieve aims I have for this group of learners?
- What elements of negotiation could I introduce?

Table 3.2 Model Two: An interactive view of the teacher's role

Issue	Teacher's role	Student's role
Information conveyed in both directions. Teaching dependent on feedback from the learner	Expert	Novice or apprentice
Control over learning process – student conceived of more as an equal partner	Facilitator/negotiator of the learning process and content of what is to be learned	Active contributions are valued (equal partners). Learner's lead may be followed or capitalised upon
Teaching dependent on the relationship between teacher and student	Developer of a relationship that will enable effective learning	Equal partner in the relationship
Context of learning	Enjoyment	Enjoyment
Responsibility for learning	Understanding of the need for learning to be in the hands of the learner	Learners take on an increasing responsibility for their own learning

Control over learning becomes negotiable, in an effort to improve its quality. Teachers and students become *equal and influential partners within the relationship*, in which their responses become the determinant of what and how learning will take place. The model does not propose classroom anarchy, but rather gives students opportunities to influence the process of learning. The clear assumption within this model is that if you give students some control, they will have a vested interest in what is learnt. If they are involved in the process of how learning takes place, then learning is much more likely to be *effective and relevant*. For students with learning difficulties it is vital we choose the approach that is in their best interests and likely to lead to the best learning outcomes .

Implicit within this role is that the teacher's role is to cultivate an interest and a sense of responsibility within students, for their own learning. They have the potential to become truly independent problem solvers. This sense of developing *autonomy* within the student is crucial.

For learning to take place there is a clear assumption in interactive approaches that it must be *enjoyable* for both parties – which assumes that there is no faking it; the mutual enjoyment must be genuine. If this is the case it will have clear implications about what and how teaching takes place. The teacher's role becomes partly one of manipulating the environment to maximise the 'fun element'.

Although difficult to define accurately, adopting this role can generate a freshness of approach on a day-to-day level that can enhance motivation. The key to its success lies in the assumption that by improving the relationship between teacher and learner the quality of teaching and learning is enhanced.

Questions to the reader

- *Is it possible to be interactive in this purist sense in all circumstances?*

  It is simply not feasible to allow negotiation of all subject matter. There will always be some aspects of the learning process that have to be suggested by teachers on the basis that they are better informed. The main issue is that teachers are aware of the different types of role they can choose, and that they understand the reasons for their choice.

- *Can I really give away control?*

  The simple answer is 'Yes', but it may be necessary to introduce moving the locus of control gradually. Students need to learn what this means and that with it comes responsibility.

- *How can adopt an interactive role in teaching students with profound and multiple learning difficulties?*

  It will be helpful at this point to read the Appendix, which clearly illustrates the teacher's role.

- *Am I doing it already?*

  Probably you are, although through examination and self-reflection it may be possible to use these roles more consciously. It is helpful to remember that some of the best language teaching takes place in relaxed, incidental situations which do not appear within the documented curriculum.

The Interactive Teacher

There exists no one view of an 'interactive teacher'. The following characteristics are presented for you to reflect upon, and compare with your existing teaching style.

Facilitator

The teacher role is to present what is to be learned in such a way that it has meaning for the learner. The teacher is there to facilitate understanding. For example, in the High/Scope approach the teacher assists and structures the learner's plans of action. The teacher firstly provides students with opportunities to choose the activity, by arranging the environment suitably. Once they identify and start to engage in a problem the teacher's role involves enabling learners to understand problems more fully, and guide them through the process towards a solution. The extent of assistance that the teacher offers is crucial and is elaborated upon further within the Scaffolder section below.

Ashman and Conway's (1993) Process-based Instruction (PBI) provides another example in which the teacher's role enables students to construct mental plans and encouraging them to think through a problem. For example, the teacher may explore different possible solutions with the students before they are tried out. Session 4 'Problem Solving' includes more discussion of PBI.

In summary, to be effective facilitators, teachers should:

- Have an internalised, flexible knowledge of learning sequences.
- Show a willingness to accept cues from students about the way in which they would like to see learning proceed, and actively use these cues in structuring the environment.
- Where appropriate, negotiate what and how learning takes place.
- Allow students to initiate learning in certain circumstances.
- Be able to present potential learning situations in a logical and understandable way for students.
- Interact in a less 'intention bound' manner. Teachers should have flexible ideas about how the task should be solved and at what rate. This skill depends very much on being in tune with the learner.
- In a general sense, value the process rather than the product of a learning opportunity.

Relationship Builder

There is an assumption that the quality of the relationship is of ultimate value, and that this determines the amount of learning that actually occurs. Learning is maximised within a dynamic, social environment. It is therefore the responsibility of teachers to ensure that relationships develop between them and their students of sufficient quality to maximise learning opportunities.

Bruner (1972) suggested that learning is not necessarily dependent on a series of skills vested in the teacher, rather within the uniqueness of the relationship.

Within this context it is vital that teachers should continually work to develop the quality of the relationship between them and their students. The development of a 'rapport' is an essential first stage which may take place within the context of a familiar routine. For example, for babies the feeding routine provides a good opportunity for early dialogue with their parents. The series of messages (offers/ acceptances/ refusals/re-negotiations) results in the development of a shared understanding between parent and baby. Such shared understandings are building blocks of effective relationships.

The teacher then works at *tuning into* the student. The assumption is that learning only occurs between them when they are really in tune. The teacher thus learns about the student through the development of their relationship.

In summary, to be effective relationship builders, teachers should:

- Positively value learners and what they are doing (teachers are not superior beings).
- Be receptive to the cues of students.
- Be familiar with the interests, likes and dislikes of the learners.
- Recognise interactive routines being established within the relationship which may form the basis of a rapport and eventually learning.
- Develop shared understandings with students which will lead to new understandings.

Reflector

Teachers are constantly learning about and modifying their relationships with students. It is an active process for both parties. For teachers this confers a responsibility to be constantly learning and re-tuning from what has gone before, returning to the learners re-briefed from each previous teaching session. The relationship will naturally change and mature. The teacher must be conscious of the implications and opportunities for learning that this brings.

In summary, to be effective reflectors, teachers should:

- Adjust their responses to the changing needs of learners.
- Constantly retune in the light of previous sessions.

Scaffolder

Bruner (1972) considered that adults should structure interactions so that children can learn from them. Initially, the expert models what is to be learnt, and this is increasingly informed by dialogue with the novice. The expert provides the novice with opportunities for learning that are just outside his or her reach (just a little too difficult) and then provides a scaffold to enable progress. Sometimes this scaffold is physical and sometimes it is verbal but essentially the expert provides the right amount of assistance for the apprentice to achieve success.

Teachers are often afraid to allow students to make mistakes, but if attention is drawn to their consequences, they are very powerful learning tools. Providing just the right amount of scaffolding following a mistake can encourage specific learning and gradually reducing this support can enable students to assume greater responsibility for their own learning. This process is further described in Session 5 'Prompting and Scaffolding'.

See also Session 2 in which the development of teaching routines forms yet another aspect of the teacher's role.

In summary, in order to be effective scaffolders, teachers should:

• Provide opportunities for learning which are just a little too difficult for the students.

• Offer just the right amount of assistance for them to enjoy the experience and thus learn from it.

• Structure learning from mistakes.

Margaret Donaldson's work with young children, built upon the work of Piaget on child development, provides a pithy quotation which can be applied to teaching and learning at any age:

> The teacher is there to guide the child towards tasks where he/she will objectively do well, but not too easily, not without putting forth some effort, not without difficulties to be mastered, errors to be overcome, creative solutions to be found.
>
> (Donaldson, 1978)

Teachers must challenge learners or they will not be stimulated to move forward in their learning. They must also be aware that they hold fundamental keys to success in the quality of teacher learner relationships.

2. Reflection

Last Session's Focus

Begin your reflection by sharing with a partner or with the group an evaluation of the action plan you made at the end of the previous session. Was it successful? What did you learn? Where might you go next in this area?

This Session's Focus

In small groups, each member of the group should place a mark on the continuum line to illustrate the extent to which they believe their teaching style:

Controls students:

Controlling   *Facilitating*

|_____|

Positively values and builds on the contribution of students:

Important   *Unimportant*

|_____|

Develops positive relationship with students:

Important   *Unimportant*

```
⌊_____⌋
```

Is facilitating rather than instructing:

Facilitating   *Instructing*

```
⌊_____⌋
```

The group should then discuss the distribution of marks on the line, and the reasons.

As individuals list the way your style is:

A   Interactive

B   Traditional

Consider in small groups how these might be developed.

3. How to move on

Make a list of those things about your current teaching style you would like to change in the following format:

Aspects of my teaching style I would like to alter	Things I am going to do in order to achieve this

4. Action plan

Plan to video yourself in a representative teaching situation to enable you to fulfil the following tasks:

- Describe exactly what you are doing.
- Judge what you think the students are learning.
- Pick out the interactive features of your teaching.
- Suggest how you might be able to improve this style.
- Make a list of other times when you feel you use an interactive style of teaching.
- Make another list of times when this style would be less appropriate.

Further Reading

Reference	Points of Interest
Ashman, A. and Conway, C. (1993) *Using Cognitive Methods in the Classroom*. London: Routledge.	Constructing mental plans
Bruner, J. (1972) *The Relevance of Education*. London: Allen & Unwin.	
Christie, P., Newson, E., Newson. J. and Prevezer, W. (1992) 'An interactive approach to language and communication for non-speaking children'. In Lane and Miller (eds) *Handbook of Child and Adolescent Therapy*. Oxford: Oxford University Press.	Examples of tuning in to the learner
Donaldson, M. (1978) *Children's Minds*. London: Fontana.	Basic text on the development of children's thinking
Jordan, J., Singh, N. and Rapp, C. (1989) 'An evaluation of gentle teaching and visual screening in reduction of stereotype', *Journal of Applied Behavioural Analysis*, **22(1)**, 9-22.	Positively valuing the learner
Nind, M. and Hewett, D. (1994) *Access to Communication: Developing the Basics of Communication with People with Severe Learning Difficulties through Intensive Interaction*. London: David Fulton Publishers	Relationship between teacher and learner

Model One: The traditional role within the teaching process

Issue	Teacher's role	Student's role
Information is conveyed in one direction	Imparter of knowledge-providing the learner with a set of directions	Receiver of information
Control over learning process	In control of the path of learning	Student follows lead
Context of learning recipient	Controller of the environment	Passive recipient

Interactive Approaches to Teaching. © Mark Collis and Penny Lacey

Model Two: An interactive view of the role

Issue	Teacher's role	Student's role
Information conveyed in both directions. Teaching dependent on feedback from the learner	Expert	Novice or apprentice
Control over learning student conceived of more as an equal partner	Facilitator/ learning process and content of what is to be learned	Active are valued (equal partners). Learner's lead may be followed or capitalised on.
Teaching dependent on the relationship between teacher and student	Developer of a relationship that will enable effective learning	Equal partners in the relationship
Context of learning	Enjoyment	Enjoyment
Responsibility for learning	Understanding of the need for learning to be in the hands of the learner	Learners take on an increasing responsibility for their own learning

Interactive Approaches to Teaching. © Mark Collis and Penny Lacey

SESSION 4

Problem Solving

Problem solving ability is essential to adult life. In this session the demands of problem solving are explored and ideas for teaching students to become effective problem solvers are suggested.

1. Focus

Problem Solving: An Attitude Towards Teaching

A problem solving approach to teaching will affect everything the teacher does. It will pervade every aspect of the curriculum and requires the teacher to take every opportunity to engage the learner in active and ultimately self-initiated problem solving. Every task the student is set or independently encounters can be seen as a challenge or 'problem' to be solved. Teaching focuses on the qualitative way in which each problem is solved. The aim becomes to assist the learner to become a more effective and independent problem solver. The curriculum becomes the means by which this is achieved. Problem solving therefore describes an attitude to teaching rather than a method that can be applied in certain circumstances.

There are many occasions when teachers automatically solve the naturally arising problems facing people with learning difficulties. We seem compelled to help, without thinking about the potential these problems have for the development of the learner as a more independent problem solver and thinker. It is important to remember that failing, in moderation, is crucial to successful learning.

Principles of a Problem Solving Approach

- Problems are continuously presenting themselves and being solved by us all in the process of everyday life. Efficient problem solving is intrinsic to functioning as an independent individual.

- All students can improve through direct teaching of thinking and problem solving. For this to happen, teaching must become more than transferring a set of skills to learners. It involves enabling them to become more efficient and independent in their thought processes. The acquisition and use of skills is thus placed within the context of a cycle of thinking and problem solving.

- The solving of any problem involves a common process. Students with learning difficulties may encounter a variety of obstacles at any stage of that cycle illustrated in the figure below. The teacher may, through a planned programme of activities, provide focused practice at the particular part of the cycle with which the student is having difficulties. For example if there is a difficulty in seeing a problem then solving it is going to be impossible. A focused educational programme designed to overcome this particular problem may be set within any existing curriculum.

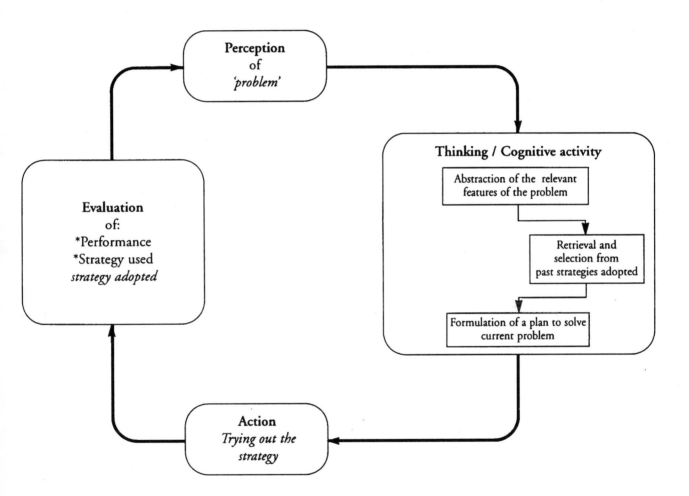

Figure 4.1 The Problem Solving Cycle

The following example illustrates the importance of developing independent problem-solving skills.

Tony wanted to make a cup of tea. He went into the kitchen to find there were no tea-bags. He stood waiting for something to happen, either for the tea-bags to appear or for someone to tell him what to do. Neither happened so he went without a drink.

In these circumstances, Tony appears to lack the strategies needed to solve the problem. It might have been that he did not realise that tea-bags were needed; that is, he did not realise that there was a problem at all. Alternatively, his difficulty could have been in selecting an appropriate strategy to solve the problem. He could have chosen to go and buy tea-bags, he could have borrowed them from somewhere else, or decided on a different drink or even asked for help. From observing Tony on several occasions, the teacher needs to decide where, within the problem solving cycle, his difficulties lie and plan appropriate intervention strategies to enable him to move forward.

Intervention Strategies

The cycle of problem solving illustrates that intervention may occur at a variety of points, as Figure 4.2 demonstrates. It may be argued that purely behavioural interventions focus solely on the 'action stage'. This should not deny the validity or effectiveness of such an approach. Indeed such methods as shaping, imitation, modelling and overcorrection undoubtedly do change behaviour. However, the problem solving approach suggests that the action stage is only part of the process and hence describes only a limited set of potential interventions.

Each of the points of intervention will now be considered individually to help teachers to understand where teaching might be effective.

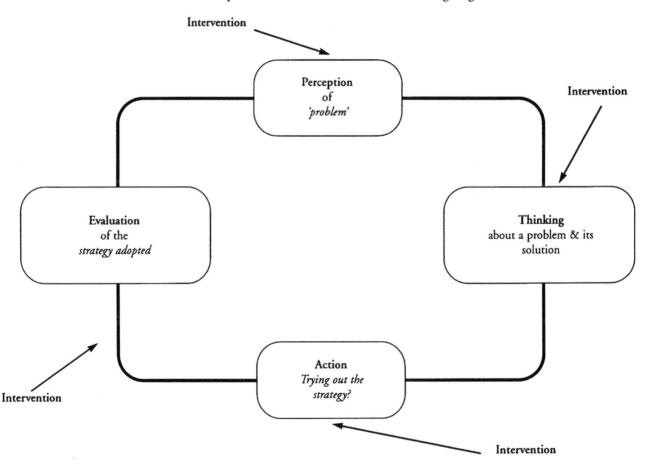

Figure 4.2 Intervention within the problem-solving cycle

Developing a perception of the problem itself
Can the learner see the problem?

The aim of teaching at this stage is to ensure the learner appreciates that a problem exists at all. Many students with learning difficulties are particularly challenged by this. Teaching must clearly be dependent on the problem being a real one for this individual learner. The teaching or intervention strategy may initially involve making the outward signs of the problem more obvious and tailoring it to the interests of the learner. To illustrate, during the making of a drink, the fact that no cups are provided may be the problem. To help the perception of this, pictures of cups are used to cue the learner into the fact that no cups means no drink.

It will be of interest to explore why the learner does not see the problem:
- Is it a physical difficulty? Is it a result of seating or positioning? If so could this be changed to make the problem more accessible?
- Is it the result of an impairment? If so could any assistance be provided?
- Is the problem being ignored rather than not being perceived at all? If so, why?
- Does he or she expect to be a passive recipient of instruction?
- Is he or she not interested in drinking?
- Does he or she have an understanding of cause and effect?

Developing the ability to break down a problem into elements
Can the learner split the problem up so that it can be done more easily
(as a sum of its parts)?

In particular, the solving of larger problems relies on them being broken down. When taken as a whole some problems may not make sense, or may not easily be accessible to be solved.

For example, cooking a meal presents a problem which will need to be broken down into steps before it can be solved. Food needs to be bought, it needs to be cooked in the right way, it must be served and eaten, then cleared up. For someone with poor sequencing or timing skills, achieving this can be very difficult. Breaking down the problem into small steps is essential before solutions can be found and much work can be done by teacher and learner to help this process. 'Recipe' cards can be used to talk through the problems before solutions are considered. This then aids the working through of the actual situation.

The learner may not perceive the problem to be complex and may want to begin on the solution before really understanding what is needed. For a 'good' solution to be found it is important that each stage is thoroughly understood before embarking on the next part of the problem solving process.

Developing the ability to abstract the relevant features of a problem

'Teaching may focus on developing an understanding that there are different parts of a problem, which when put together may give some insight into its solution. This may involve encouraging selective attention to those features of a problem that will assist the production of a plan to solve it.

It may prove more crucial to take into account certain features of a problem rather than others. When faced with an overflowing sink, the problem itself has a variety of features (e.g. water collects on the floor, items of washing up may float on top of the water, as the water falls it splashes your shoes; however, it is crucial the solver focuses on those that are most relevant or meaningful (e.g. both taps are full on and the plug is in). If this does not happen, strategies may be formed that do not directly tackle the problem.

Many students with autism find this part of the cycle particularly challenging and may need considerable support and practice at isolating the relevant features.

Developing an ability to find meaning in these features

For example, a problem was constructed by the teacher who, suggesting a birthday party, provided everything but the chairs. The students might recognise that something is wrong. This must be followed by a realisation that the objects we normally use for sitting on are not there and therefore ask the question, 'What are we going to sit on?'. However, they could also ask, 'Do we need to sit?'. It might be that chairs are not in fact needed on this occasion. This example tries to show that there is a need to think further about the nature of the problem before engaging in any planning. Indeed students may easily rush at creating a solution before having clearly considered the meaning of the features of the problem.

There are times when this may involve the grouping or 'chunking' of the features of a problem. It is suggested that many people with learning difficulties have problems in this area. However, they will need to have opportunities to learn that when features of a particular problem are combined they may have a special meaning. For example, if a student has no clean clothes to wear this may have special relevance when taken together with the fact that she is also going out to dinner tonight. In this way context starts to become a feature of the problem and when combined with existing features changes the nature of the problem. In this case, the evening out will influence which clothes the student will wash and how quickly she will have to have them ready.

Developing a plan to solve a problem

Process Based Instruction (PBI) as described by Ashman and Conway (1993) demonstrates how plans can be formulated to assist a student to deal with almost any eventuality. The authors do suggest that those with more serious learning difficulties may find the concept of a plan difficult to grasp. However once established, they can use and apply the planning process.

Figure 4.3 illustrates how a Makaton symbol plan could assist a student to prepare a simple recipe. Each page has a separate symbol, which at the early stages is accompanied by a picture to assist the cueing-in process. Again, early on there would only be two or three pages to describe the whole process and this would be gradually extended so that the task required less and less adult assistance.

	Step one
	Step two
	Step three
	Step four
	Step five

Figure 4.3 Symbol plan to assist in preparing a simple recipe

Developing a way of remembering how to solve a problem

The student must remember a plan long enough to employ it. This may be achieved by, for example, using strategies such as rehearsal, or visualisation, or the development of scripts. The latter may take the form of tangible reminders to the student of how to solve a particular problem or set of problems. For example a sequence of Makaton symbols drawn on a strip of card may be sufficient to remind a student of a possible plan to solve the cup problem.

The strategy adopted would obviously have to be tailored to the level of understanding of the student.

Developing the students' ability to evaluate their attempts to carry out plans

A chance to evaluate is crucial to the success of future attempts at the task, or related tasks. The student can be helped to structure this process, so that maximum benefit can be gleaned for his or her own attempt to solve the original problem. To illustrate with reference to our example the student may be asked:

• What was the effect of the strategy you employed?

• Were you able to produce the drink you wanted?

• Can you think of any other ways of achieving a 'better' result?

The learner is encouraged throughout to attain increasingly higher levels of independence in aspects of solving the problem. The reader is advised to reflect again on the above when engaged in Session 5 'Prompting and Scaffolding.'

Problem solving approaches that draw on this basic cycle

Two models of teaching and learning which draw directly on a problem solving approach are:

- High/Scope (Hohmann, Banet and Weikart, 1979). This model is as much a classroom organisation model as a theory of teaching. It centres around a Plan-do-review cycle of organising activity (see Session 5).
- PBI (Process Based Instruction) – Ashman and Conway (1993). This model, described briefly above, aims to improve the means by which the student attacks and solve problems (often co-operatively). Students are encouraged to use plans, which are defined as sequences of thought or activity that will lead to success on a specific task. Effectively, these are designed to assist the student to form a mental representation or picture of the problem.

Factors to bear in mind when designing a problem

The extent and the way in which the teacher manipulates the process of solving the problem must be carefully considered. Some of the following points may be worth bearing in mind:

- It is crucial to design the task carefully so that it provides particular practice on that area of development needed by the student.
- It is also important to consider how much the teacher should control the process, the strategies and the solutions the learner generates. This will vary according to the ability and stage of development of individual students.
- For those least able learners, in particular those students with profound and multiple learning difficulties, whose total amount of learning may be limited, it is important to choose functionally relevant problems. For example it may be relevant to work on an effective means of gaining an adult's attention when he or she needs a drink. This can pose problems for teachers (see Example 2 below).
- The task should challenge the learner. It should not be so easy that the learner solves it without thought or perhaps by simply adopting a well-tried strategy. Yet it should not be so difficult as to destroy the confidence of the learners and cause them to give up trying. Only careful observation and deep knowledge of the abilities of students can help teachers get the amount of challenge right.

From these examples it can be seen that many problems are posed quite naturally and teachers must seize these opportunities to challenge their students to think for themselves. It is tempting to maintain control over every situation and difficult to stand back and give over responsibility but if students with learning difficulties are ever to become effective problem solvers they must be presented with situations where genuine thinking is needed.

Example 1

Mr Brown was working with a small group of students who were capable of solving problems with several stages providing each stage was presented separately. From assessing the working through of previous problems set, Mr Brown realised that he needed to provide opportunities for the students to see the consequences of forgetting to perform a step within their solution. Usually he stopped them and through questioning helped them to remember what to do next so that the problem was successfully solved. He decided to let them make mistakes and then build up again from this point.

Their first mistake was made when they were expected to be able to share out the food at dinner time. The student with responsibility that day failed to deal out the available food fairly so that there was nothing left for the last two plates. At first the two students without food made no comment but eventually another student noticed they were not eating. Mr Brown still refrained from interfering and waited to see what was going to happen. In fact nothing happened and these two students went without any food.

The lesson could not, however, stop there. After dinner, Mr Brown sat with the group and talked through with them what had happened. He encouraged the students to re-enact the scene and took instant photographs of the two students with sad faces. He then helped them all to think of a way of getting some food for those who were still hungry. The real learning was to take place on the next day. Before dinner Mr Brown got out the photographs of the hungry students and just asked everyone to remember what happened. He was prepared to point to the pictures again when the food was being dealt out but it was not necessary. He knew, however, that he would have to provide the reminder strategy many times at future mealtimes before every member of the group had internalised it.

Example 2

John is a young student with cerebral palsy and profound learning difficulties. He is very interested in people and in watching all that is happening around him. He appears to understand simple cause and effect and to understand some of what people say to him. He is particularly adept at smiling and laughing appropriately. However, he only ever reacts to other people and never initiates communication. His teacher wants to find a way to encourage him to recognise the need to ask for attention. She stands in front of John with her back to him and moves close to him so that she touches his hand. 'Oh John' she says as she swings round, 'what do you want?'. She repeats this many times. She also responds to any slight noises that John makes as if he is asking for attention. Gradually she encourages him to understand that he can begin a 'conversation' between himself and another person. It is a very slow process and John does not use his ability to attract someone's attention very often.

John is at a very early stage of problem solving. His teacher is fairly sure that he is not really aware that he has a problem to solve. He is• content with his extremely passive life. Food, drink, and entertainment come to him without much effort and he does not see the necessity to pull someone's arm or use his voice to make something happen. His teacher is trying to break this passivity and encourage him to take a little control of his own life.

2. Reflection

Last Session's Focus

Begin your reflection by sharing with a partner or with the group an evaluation of the action plan that you made at the end of the previous session. Was it successful? What did you learn? Where might you go next in this area?

This Session's Focus

This activity is designed to encourage you to discuss the different aspects of this session. In small groups:

• Think of a student you work with. What type of problems do you think he or she cannot identify? Why?

• Generate one example of a problem that this student would have significant difficulties in solving.

• Are there any other stages at which s/he would have difficulties? What are they? How could you check this?

3. How to move on

Discuss the following questions in your group.

1. How can functional problems be presented within the context of your own situation? How can they be incorporated into the day?

2. How can the curriculum reflect a problem solving approach? Which aspect or subject would best lend itself to it?

Decide ways in which you are going to begin developing the curriculum.

4. Action plan

Return to the student you identified in the reflection section and plan a focused programme of problem solving activities to give him or her more practice at this particular aspect of the cycle.

Consider how you can carry out the plan on the student for whom it was designed so that you can answer the following questions:

• Did the plan assist the student?

• Was it a useful strategy to provide for the learner?

• Could it be changed to help him or her?

• What effect do you think it could have in the long term?

• How could similar plans help the student solve problems?

Further Reading	Reference	Points of Interest
	Ashman, A. and Conway, R. (1993) *Using Cognitive Methods in the Classroom.* London: Routledge.	Planning
	Jordan, R. and Powell, S.(1991) 'Teaching thinking: the case for principles', *European Journal of Special Needs Education,* **6**(2), 112-123.	Teaching thinking
	Hohmann, M., Banet, B. and Weikart, D. (1979) *Young Children in Action.* Ypsilanti, Michigan: High/Scope Press.	High/Scope – a cognitive oriented curriculum

The problem solving process

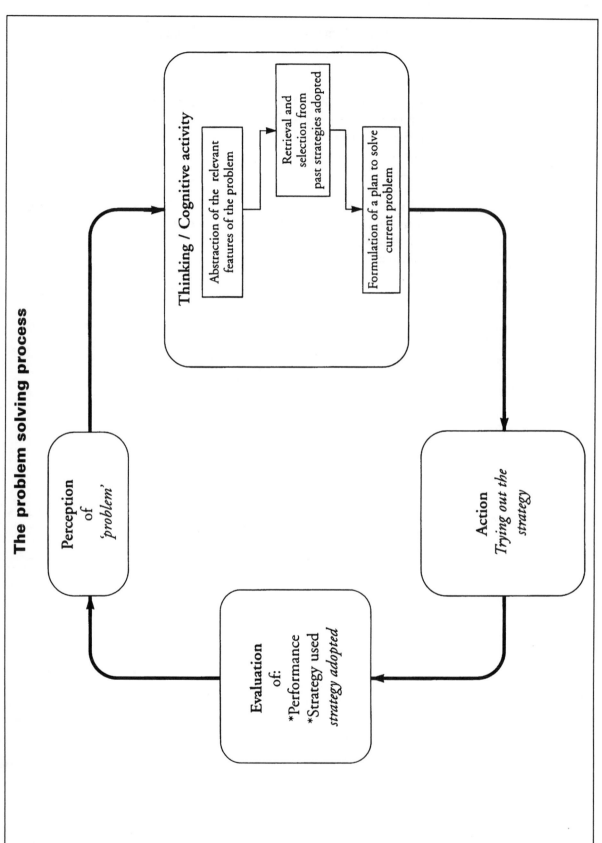

Interactive Approaches to Teaching. © Mark Collis and Penny Lacey

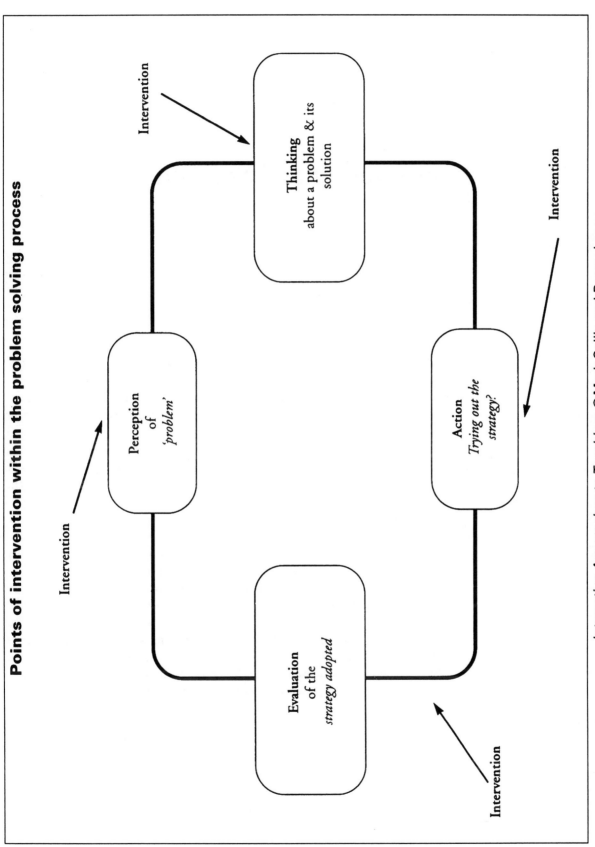

Points of intervention within the problem solving process

Thinking
about a problem & its
solution

Intervention

Perception
of
'problem'

Intervention

Action
*Trying out the
strategy?*

Intervention

Evaluation
of the
strategy adopted

Intervention

Interactive Approaches to Teaching. © Mark Collis and Penny Lacey

SESSION 5

Prompting and Scaffolding

The intention in this session is to explore the nature of interactive prompting and how the quality of the interaction between teacher and learner can determine the quality and diversity of the learning that occurs.

1. Focus

Think of someone learning to drive a car. The instructor spends the first few lessons talking through every aspect of turning on the engine, depressing the clutch, selecting the appropriate gear, using the mirror etc. The learner is given an enormous amount of verbal support as he or she practises the different aspects of driving. Gradually as the lessons go by, the learner is given fewer and fewer specific instructions but the instructor might ask questions such as, 'What do you have to do before you pull out?' or 'We're going to turn right at the next junction, what do you need to think about' Later the instructor might not ask questions to check the answer is correct but just simply say, 'Start thinking through your approach list now.' The learner is at the stage where he or she can be trusted to get it right once he or she has had a gentle reminder. Eventually the instructor withdraws altogether and the learner can remember the strategies taught and can apply them in any traffic situation.

This example illustrates the way in which an *expert* can provide the necessary support for a *novice* to move from dependence to independence in a highly complex situation. (An expert has been defined as 'a more capable other who takes the novice or apprentice through the learning situation'.) The prompts change as the learner becomes more skillful. First of all there are very full verbal prompts and even perhaps some physical prompts on gear changing. Later these are handed over to the learner who is encouraged to create lists of reminders for manoeuvres (Figure 5.1).

Assistance

It is important that the expert provides the assistance that is directly related to the amount of help needed by the novice to complete the task. Through giving instructions, demonstrating or direct prompting the expert takes control of the

```
┌──────────────────────────────────────────────────────────────┐
│                    Expert fully supports novice              │
│         demonstration/ physical manipulation through task     │
└──────────────────────────────────────────────────────────────┘
                              │
                              ▼
┌──────────────────────────────────────────────────────────────┐
│                 Expert shares control with novice             │
│                   expert provides plan for novice             │
│                         physical prompts                      │
│                         gestural prompts                      │
│                          verbal prompts                       │
└──────────────────────────────────────────────────────────────┘
                              │
                              ▼
┌──────────────────────────────────────────────────────────────┐
│                Expert hands over control to novice            │
│                 expert negotiates plan with novice            │
│                      reminds novice of plan                   │
│                  provides feedback on performance             │
└──────────────────────────────────────────────────────────────┘
                              │
                              ▼
┌──────────────────────────────────────────────────────────────┐
│                       Novice takes control                    │
│            expert observes but has 'hands off'                │
│                      novice uses own plan                     │
│                    self-checks its effectiveness              │
│     expert may need to make suggestions to enable lateral thinking │
│        expert provides feedback until it is no longer necessary │
└──────────────────────────────────────────────────────────────┘
```

Figure 5.1

parts of the task which the novice cannot complete alone. As competence increases more of the task is handed over to the novice until she or he can perform alone. Sometimes the novice needs very specific assistance but at other times general help is sufficient.

Gauging just the right amount of assistance is challenging for the expert as it can be very tempting to over-help the learner so that she or he does not fail at each task. The teacher's job is to guide learners towards tasks where they will be able to succeed in their objective, but not too easily. There must be some difficulties to be mastered, errors to be overcome and creative solutions to be found. There is an enormous amount of learning that can be done through making mistakes. In the example of learning to drive, the expert has to make instant judgements concerning the kind of mistakes she or he can let the learner make. Some mistakes could be fatal and dual-control brakes are very important to prevent these. There are, however, many other kinds of mistakes which are less dangerous and these can be very powerful learning aids. The learner needs to crunch the gears a few times to get the feel of how to avoid that and change smoothly.

One of the important features of experts providing carefully gauged assistance is the fact that learners can tackle tasks that are too difficult for them to do alone. The expert is providing the necessary scaffolding for them to climb to new heights. The principle gives the opportunity for learners at a very early stage of development to be involved in quite complicated tasks even though they can only complete a small part of the task alone. Involvement, however, must be genuine. It is easy for it to become tokenistic as, for example, when a person with profound and multiple learning disabilities is placed in the kitchen and a meal is cooked around him or her. Real involvement in the task demands a high degree of knowledge of that learner's strengths and needs, the level of understanding which can be achieved in that situation and the exact stage at which assistance is necessary.

Choosing the Task

Sharing task between experts and learners is only an effective learning tool if the task chosen is slightly too difficult for the learner to solve alone. If it is too easy or too difficult the learner will gain little from the exercise. The support given by the expert must be eventually transferrable to the learner or she or he will never be able to perform the task alone nor transfer the learning to novel tasks. The plans featured in the previous session are important to remember at this point as powerful strategies for the eventual handing over of control to the learner. It contains an element of risk, as does teaching someone to drive a car, but the rewards are great when independence is achieved.

It has already been suggested that students will find learning easier and more interesting if the task chosen is of fundamental interest to them. It is not always possible to match this completely because some students become obsessed by one particular topic and find it difficult to initiate something new. But in general, the task chosen should be as close to the learner's present functioning as possible, especially when working with students with learning difficulties who will usually progress at a very slow rate.

At this point, it is worth considering how to work with students who seem completely wrapped up in their own worlds of self-stimulation. Traditional thinking supports using behaviour modification to extinguish the unwanted behaviour to enable new, more constructive behaviours to emerge. More recent ideas would suggest beginning with the behaviours already used by the student, believing them to have an important function for that person. Helping them to move on would include using those behaviours. For example, a student who hand flaps, perhaps to produce some kind of predictable order to a world he cannot understand, can be encouraged to interact with members of staff if they join him in handflapping in front of their own faces. The student is encouraged to notice the face and to begin to respond to exaggerated expressions. It is a long process but is a genuine attempt by staff to enter the world of the student and work from where he is rather than introducing completely arbitrary tasks a long way from his understanding. There are, however, some challenging behaviours which would be dangerous to treat as starting points for teaching and careful discussion will be needed to agree where this line lies.

Prompting

Prompting has been mentioned several times as a strategy for supporting learners. It is usual to connect prompting with strict behavioural techniques as the trainer shapes the trainee's behaviour closer to the desired performance. Prompting within an interactive framework is both similar and different. At the beginning of learning a new task or with a learner at an early stage of development, prompts may be very specific with a desired end in mind, but as the learner becomes more competent the prompts can become more generalised, for example 'What do you think you should do first?' 'Try it and see what happens?' 'Did it work?'. These kinds of prompts hand over the control to the learner. The expert does not necessarily have a fixed idea of the end point and is encouraging the learner to employ his or her own thinking with the express aim of helping to improve the thinking itself.

Questioning has already been mentioned as a useful teaching tool in Session 2. Questions provide good possibilities for assisting students to think for themselves and become self-regulatory in their performance. Consider this exchange between student and teacher:

S. What are we doing this afternoon?

T. Can you think what it might be?

S. No.

T. What day is it today?

S. Tuesday.

T. Can you remember what we usually do on a Tuesday afternoon?

S. No.

T. Can you think where you can look to find out?

S. No.

T. How about on the timetable?

S. Oh Yes.

(*S.* goes to the timetable)

T. Which day is Tuesday?

S. That one.

T. Which bit is afternoon?

S. That bit.

T. So what are we doing this afternoon?

S. Swimming.

The teacher is encouraging the student to become more independent by taking her through the sequence which will enable her to find out the information she needs on her own another time. If this sequence is repeated enough times, eventually the prompts can become more vague:

S. What are we doing this afternoon?

T. How can you find out?

S. From the timetable

It is hoped that the sequence through which the teacher took the student can become an inner conversation so that she can think what day it is and find the right section on the timetable to reveal what is going to happen.

For learners who are not yet able to respond to verbal prompts in this way, physical or gestural prompts can be employed. It is more difficult for these kinds of prompts to enable creative thinking on the part of the learner but some of the process is evident. Consider, for example a learner at the stage of simple turn-taking games.

The teacher begins a game involving the exchange of a catalogue between him and the student. He knows that this is a popular game with that particular student but that she needs considerable prompting to become engaged. The teacher spends several turns placing the catalogue in the student's hands and removing it again. He does this in an exaggerated and teasing manner using his face to demonstrate enjoyment, feigning surprise at losing the catalogue and relief when he takes it back again. After this initial highly prompted section of the game, the student begins to join in and gradually takes over, controlling the timing and the finishing of the game. She has become engaged and is beginning to use simple thought processes to keep the social interaction going.

Cognitive Strategies

If we return to the teacher in the first example in the previous section we can appreciate that she is helping the student to learn to use cognitive strategies to aid thinking. There has been a considerable interest in thought processes and how students can be encouraged to be more aware of the ways in which they think, understand and remember things. This has been given the name 'metacognition' which literally means 'thinking about thinking'. Normally developing children begin to develop simple plans and strategies for solving problems at a very young age. Their first strategies tend to be trial and error but gradually they begin to learn from previous experience and from the assistance offered by adults. Students with learning difficulties appear to find particular difficulty in developing their own strategies and need specific help in acquiring them.

Using memory strategies to aid recall of relevant information provides good examples of improving ways to approach novel tasks. Such strategies include rehearsal, grouping or chunking, visual imagery and verbal elaboration. Consider trying to remember a new telephone number. How do you do it? Do you keep repeating it over and over again or do you divide into two sets of three numbers or three sets of two numbers or do you make them make a sum together or do you invent a 'story' for them (e.g., a story to remember 217648 might be 21 because I'm not 21, 76 because my daughter was born then and 48 because that was when was born)! We all have different strategies but we have devised one which works for us. Many people with learning difficulties need to be led through the process of understanding why this should be necessary and how to devise something that works for them.

Playing games such as 'Kim's Game' and 'Granny went to market and she bought...' can help generally to improve memory but if students with learning difficulties are going to transfer that to natural situations then more overt teaching of the strategies is going to be necessary. Remembering items on a shopping list can be achieved through encouraging visual imagery. This can be done first with actual objects, then with pictures, then with symbols or words and finally by asking the students to think of the image of the object. The teacher can be prompting appropriately throughout until the students can use the strategy independently when it is needed.

Plan-do-review

Another scaffold which can be overtly provided and gradually handed over to students is associated with the sequence, plan-do-review. This is a central feature of the pre-school programme pioneered in the States in the 1970s called High/Scope but it has wider applications than just that age group and can be used to encourage students of all ages to develop initiative, responsibility and independence.

Evaluation might involve a similar sheet or the possibility of annotating the plan. For instance on the first plan there might be room for a drawing or a photograph of the student playing the game with a comment on how well she or he played. If possible, the student should be encouraged to articulate what she or he felt was learned during the session and what should be learned next. This is very demanding both cognitively and linguistically and many students with learning difficulties may not progress much further than merely recalling what they did and whether they enjoyed doing it.

Plan

In the first part of the sequence the student devises a plan of action. At its simplest, students can use two objects/ symbols to choose whether to play in the water or dig in the garden but more able students will be able to choose from an array of alternatives and plan in detail what they intend to do.

Do

The second part of the sequence is carrying out the plan, which can be fleeting or intensive depending upon the ability of the students.

Review

The final part is reviewing was has happened. For some students this might mean merely pointing to where the activity took place or an object made but more able students could give a spoken or written evaluation of what happened and what could happen next time. Teacher questioning can be utilised at all stages of the procedure.

Student Work Plans

Student work plans can include details concerning the purpose of their intentions. Simple written or symbol plans might include:

• Today I will play a game using counting.

More complex plans will encourage students to set themselves more specific tasks:

• I want to learn about life in granny's day.
• I expect I will need six lessons to work on this.
• I will use the pictures on the wall, library books and I will talk to granny.
• I will start with finding out about the clothes she wore.
• I will find pictures of clothes like hers and photocopy them.
• I will talk about my work to Mr A on Friday.

Although we have spent some time illustrating possible written plans, it is not expected that every session should include this amount of detail. Most planning and reviewing will be spoken and will be fairly fleeting. It is good, occasionally, to take the planning and reviewing and develop them as processes which, with teaching, will gradually improve.

Achieving independence

The goal throughout this session has been to explore possible ways of encouraging independence in learning for students with learning difficulties. There are many times when this must be a deliberate act on the part of teachers who must be prepared to relinquish some of their control. Normally developing students usually grasp every opportunity to show how they can accomplish something on their own but that does not necessarily happen with students who experience difficulties. They may have a background of failures or of learned helplessness which discourages them from even trying. Although it may be quicker and easier to keep students in a passive role, it is not preparing them well for future independence, remembering, of course, that none of us is truly independent from the help of others. People are sociable creatures and it is right that we should all rely on each other to a certain extent.

2. Reflection

Last Session's Focus

Begin your reflection by sharing with a partner or with the group an evaluation of the action plan that you made at the end of the previous session. Was it successful? What did you learn? Where might you want to go next in this area?

This Session's Focus

(a) Agree, with a partner or small group, an example of an activity that contains several stages, appropriate to the learners with whom you work. Using the sheet entitled 'Handing over Control to Students' (Session 5, OHP 1), discuss the ways in which you can support learners whilst handing over control to them. Remember the principles of interactive approaches as you work and provide plenty of opportunities for negotiating with the learners, allowing them to make mistakes, giving them choices, giving them responsibilities and capitalising on their interests.

(b) Now take a small element of that activity and consider in detail how you will make sure that the assistance you are giving is exactly matched to the needs of the learners. This will inevitably be different for different learners.

(c) Finally, discuss the prompts you would give to support but eventually hand over control to the learners that you have in mind.

3. Moving on

List some examples from your own teaching when you make use of the prompting and scaffolding that have been the subject of this session. Extract from that list the principles you are trying to work to (e.g., giving choices, asking questions, giving clues, etc.).

Now consider where you feel you need to improve your own abilities to provide appropriate scaffolding or increase the opportunities for encouraging your learners to develop problem solving skills. List these and share them with your partner or group.

4. Action Plan

Choose one activity that lends itself well to problem solving and which is possible to carry out during the intervening time between this and the next session (e.g., cookery, gardening or going on visits) and plan how you are going to tackle it, giving yourself the opportunity to practise handing control over to your learners so that they can use their own ideas for solving problems. It may be that you can use the example you discussed with your partner/group in the reflection section. Be prepared to report back briefly at the start of the next session.

Further Reading

Reference	Points of Interest
Donaldson, M. (1978) *Children's Minds*. London: Fontana.	Basic text on the development of children's thinking
Hohmann, M., Banet, B. and Weikhart, D. (1979) *Young Children in Action*. Ypsilanti: High/Scope Press.	Developing the thinking of young children; teachers providing scaffolding
Staff of Rectory Paddock School (1983) *In Search of a Curriculum*. Sidcup: Robin Wren Publications.	Examples of teaching cognitive strategies

Tharp, R. and Gallimore,R. (1988) *Rousing Minds to Life: Teaching, Learning, and Schooling in Social Context.* Cambridge: Cambridge University Press.	Assisted performance
Wood, D. (1989) *How Children Think and Learn.* Oxford: Blackwell.	Discussion of the main ideas of psychologists who were interested in the importance of social interaction for learning, such as Bruner and Vygotsky

HANDING OVER CONTROL TO STUDENTS

1. Teacher fully supports students

2. Teacher shares control with students

3. Teacher hands over control to students

4. Students take control

Interactive Approaches to Teaching. © Mark Collis and Penny Lacey

SESSION 6

Assessment

We make a variety of assumptions about why and how we assess based on 'how we always do it'. This session calls for us to stand back from our existing practices and re-evaluate why we are assessing the student and what we are really trying to get out of it?

1. Focus

Before beginning any assessment, it is useful to ask:

- What am I assessing and why?
- What evidence is valuable for us to collect in order to determine and affect the learning situation?
- How can we best obtain this evidence?
- Once obtained, how can we use this information to influence the teaching situation directly?
- Who needs to know the results of the assessment?

What are the Purposes of Assessment?

It is vital that assessment is fundamentally to improve the quality of teaching and learning. Only too easily can it develop a life of its own, with a certain detachment from the rest of the teaching/learning process. We would propose that it is necessary continually to challenge the value and purposes of the assessments we are performing. It is helpful to consider the two main purposes of assessment for teaching and learning, *formative and summative:*

- *Formative assessment* refers to gathering information to plan the continuing process of teaching and learning. This will be a detailed picture of the student's progress and where learning is taking place.
- *Summative assessment* refers to the provision of an overall picture of a student's progress and achievements at any one point in time. This may for example be for annual review or for transition purposes.

It is very difficult for one kind of assessment to fulfil both these purposes because whichever is chosen will tend to dominate. For example using developmental checklists for both summing up progress and informing teaching encourages teachers to follow the checklist rigidly rather than looking more carefully at students' actual needs. Thus it is important to be clear about why and what we are assessing.

An interactive perspective can prompt a teacher to consider the student's:

- learning style

- interests

- motivations

- level of understanding and knowledge

- level of flexibility to meet different learning challenges

- performance in real situations

Example

Mrs Smith set up a learning situation where she could assess the progress of a group of students while they were constructing different shapes using a variety of building materials. The prompt list to guide her observations and questioning included:

- Shapes made.

- Materials used.

- Sequence of construction.

- Amount of planning.

- Level of working with others.

- Assistance needed.

- Understanding of shape.

Mrs Smith worked alongside the students, offering assistance when necessary, observing what they actually did, making judgements about their levels of understanding and gathering evidence to support her judgements. After the session, she sat with the group to record the results of the assessment. Each student was encouraged to express his or her opinion thus further refining her original judgements.

What is the potential contribution of an interactive assessment?

Following this example, it will be helpful to probe in more detail the effect of considering assessment from an interactive point of view. We are suggesting that taking this approach will enhance the quality and relevance of the whole assessment exercise.

An interactive approach to assessment should:

- *Focus on the student's level of real understanding* – Assessment should provide insight into what students actually know and how they can actually employ that knowledge. Understanding can relate to specific elements of knowledge, for example 'why we should put a coat on when it is raining'. Or it can be construed in terms of a wider ability to understand and think through problems in general. The level of understanding should therefore be clearly identified. In these terms assessment is about setting a variety of planned tasks, in an effort to see how the learner approaches them.

Assessment becomes a process of seeking *evidence of understanding.* Illustrating this evidence is implicitly more difficult than the highly replicable 'behavioural evidence'. The teacher's job becomes one of setting up learning situations in which evidence of understanding can be produced by the learner. Structuring this process becomes the challenge. Although we have stressed the importance of planning assessment opportunities, teachers must also be sufficiently flexible and alert to students providing evidence of learning at unexpected moments.

- *Provide a whole picture of the current functioning of learners,* as well as providing lists of abilities. Assessment is not just about the individual sub-tasks that learners can complete, but about providing full pictures in terms of their needs. For example, different students will have different learning styles and they will be motivated by a variety of things. Their learning experiences will be varied as will their flexibility of thought. Collecting all these together will provide a broader and more valid picture of the students' levels of learning and their abilities to take on new information.

- *Be rooted in what the learner needs to know.* Assessment should provide information to enable effective planning to meet the real challenges of students' future lives. The teacher may, for example visualise the student in 10 year's time (although this should not limit expectations of progress) and then using this as a basis for the development of a learning programme. This logic may be described as *top-down.*

Similarly an ecological view of assessment would suggest that the teacher should take a wider picture of the influences on the student's life. For example assessment at school or centre should take into account the student's home or respite situations and learning needs. When teachers formulated learning targets in the past they may have been significantly influenced by the 'next step' in a pre-determined curriculum. An interactive perspective would suggest a wider view of need. In part this builds on the last point, and suggests that the reason (the 'why' of assessment), the method (the 'how' of assessment) and the content (the 'what' of assessment) should all be guided by this perspective of what students will need in their wider and future lives.

- *Question the ownership of assessment* – Should this rest with the teacher or learner? To what extent will students be active in the assessment process? Assessment is often something that is done to them. If the teacher takes on the role of a facilitator does this imply an opportunity for the student to be more in control of the assessment processes? Information gathered becomes subject to negotiation and in so doing may well be significantly enhanced. The process of adapting Records of Achievement for students with learning difficulties has encouraged many educationists to come to terms with this issue. It is worth attempting to apply this same challenge in other areas of assessment.

- *Be an attempt to monitor the process of doing a task as much as the product of that task* – Such process-based assessment gives qualitative descriptions of how tasks are performed. This will give an indication of how the learner tackles a whole variety of different problems. For example a prompt list concentrating on how the student performs a task should include categories to provide evidence of students' planning, thinking and action.

- *Question the styles of learning that the student shows* – Assessment should ask 'how does the student learn best'? For example, does this individual learner prefer tasks to be broken down into minute steps through which she or he can progress or would she or he prefer successive presentations of the whole task?

- *Be descriptive of the learner* – This issue relates to the style of recording. Assessment may benefit from a vivid portrayal of the learning accomplished by the student that is simply not possible using checklists.

Descriptions provide the opportunity for:

(a) Assessment to become more accessible. A wider range of related professionals and importantly parents or carers can understand what learners can do and what they are going to do next.

(b) Giving an overall picture of the learner which may not be possible through breaking individual skills down into their sub-component parts.

(c) Account for progress in areas such as knowledge, understanding, interest and motivation.

(d) Provide evidence for teachers' judgements about students' progress.

This will necessarily have an effect on the design of assessment sheets. A series of prompt statements (to remind teachers of what they are looking for) would be followed by comment boxes (to enable teachers to write concise descriptions of what they saw and heard). This is explored further later in this session.

What should be the assessment focus?

Assessment should focus on both the *learner* and the *environment* and the relationship between them.

Traditional task-analysis suggests that the learner is of secondary importance to the task whereas interactive approaches values the relationship between the two. Assessment should focus on the learner's perceptions, strategies and interests in relation to the task. This suggests a learner-analysis, which can be neatly contrasted to the more traditional task-analysis. The task cannot be coldly separated from the learner, as it is the means by which the learner acts on the task which is important to ascertain. The learner is the focus.

The characteristics of the learner will have a major influence on the rate and level of learning.

Assessment can also focus on aspects of the environment. There are several angles to this:

- The nature of the task.
- The context.
- Available resources.
- Social relationships.
- The amount of assistance needed to complete the task.

This involves assessment at a variety of different levels:

(a) The learner's current level of acquired knowledge and skills.

(b) The learner's preferred learning style.

(c) Affective considerations e.g. mood, motivation and co-operation.

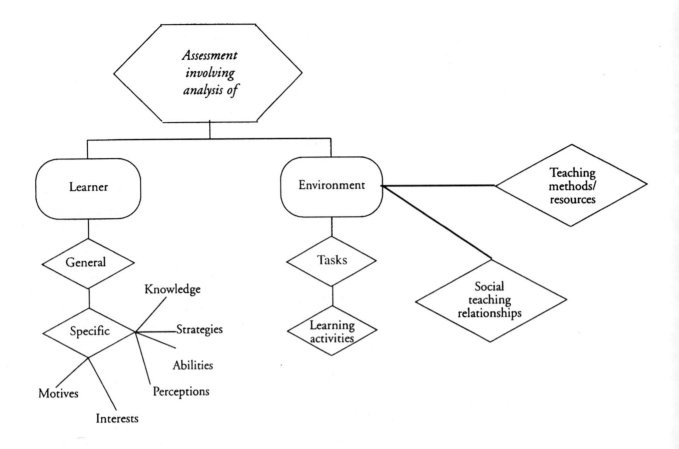

Figure 6.1 (taken from Norwich, 1993)

The phrase *Dynamic Assessment* (Feuerstein, Rand and Hoffman, 1979) has been coined as a term to describe one approach to an ecological assessment. The word dynamic indicates a contrast with the usual kind of static assessment where the student is examined at a particular point in time focusing on the product of learning. Dynamic assessment provides insight into the processes the learner is using which contributes to a total picture of his or her functioning.

This kind of assessment can describe the potential of the learner as it can identify some of the skills and understanding that lie just outside the current range of abilities. It can focus on enabling the student to reach this next stage of learning by analysing the nature and amount of assistance required to complete the task. This has been called *Assisted Assessment* (Campione, 1989) and implies sound knowledge of appropriate assistance (see Session 5 'Prompting and Scaffolding') and the ability to observe carefully the learning that is taking place.

The learner is observed performing to his or her highest ability independently then again when receiving assistance to see how much further she or he can go. The gap between the independent and assisted performances is the *zone of next development* and it indicates where teaching will be most effective.

Assessment Techniques

Assessment techniques include:

- Tests.
- Checklists.
- Schedules.
- Questioning.
- Observation.

The two most important within an interactive context are questioning and observation.

Questioning

Questioning is a traditional mainstay of the assessment and teaching process. Good teachers can use questioning both to find out what students already know and to direct them into understanding new concepts. However, many teachers overuse lower order questions which merely demand recall, for example:

- What's this?
- What colour is the cup?
- Who told the footballer to take the penalty?
- Where did the old woman live?

To encourage students' deeper thinking it is necessary for teachers to ask questions which encourage speculation, analysis and evaluation such as:

- What would happen if you poured water onto this?
- Why did the car have to stop so quickly?
- How difficult do you think you are going to find that?

Many students with learning difficulties find it a problem to answer questions which encourage them to think. They are often well used to responding to recall and naming questions but need considerable practice at the higher order questions. Teachers need to give students plenty of practice and also to demonstrate how to answer thinking questions:

> 'How does this work? I think I'll try this out first. Ah yes, it works if you push it backwards first.'

> 'I want to find out why we can see the moon in the daytime. Does anyone know why we can? No? Well, let's start with this book...'

An ultimate goal is to get students to ask questions themselves as these can effectively reveal their thinking.

Of course, there are many students with learning difficulties who are unable to answer even the most simple questions either because of lack of understanding or because of a communication disability.

Observation

Good observation is essential to interactive assessment. A picture of students' abilities and achievements can be built up over time using observation to provide examples of evidence of learning.

Although some aspects can be pre-decided, basically this observation must be open-ended in design. Too many pre-conceived ideas will lead to the observer missing valuable pieces of information. Manageability must be weighed up against this open-ended nature. It is impossible to observe everything. Somehow the observer must be directed towards what to look for.

Prompt sheets are useful tools as they provide broad areas within which to obtain evidence of learning. They are less restricting than checklists which can discourage observers from recording what is actually happening. A prompt sheet in the area of reading might look like this (adapted from Barrs et al., 1988).

- overall impression of student's reading

- confidence and degree of independence

- involvement in the book/text

- the way in which the student reads the text aloud

Strategies the student uses when reading aloud
drawing on previous experience to make sense of the text
using book language
reading the pictures
focusing on print
using semantic/syntactic/grapho-phonic clues
predicting
self-correcting
using several strategies or over-dependent on one

Student's response to text
personal response
critical response (understanding, appreciating wider meanings)

These broad areas have the effect of directing the teacher to ascertain what learning the student is actually demonstrating in reading. It encourages short narrative records and examples rather than ticks. Further analysis can be carried out following this using the principles of dynamic assessment, which will enable a closer look at the strategies the student can be encouraged to use when assistance is offered.

Observation is a particularly crucial tool when assessing students who are at a very early stage of development. Using video to record what is happening can be helpful as it can be run repeatedly to scrutinise the smallest actions. There are a few assessment schedules, based on interactive principles, which have been found to be useful for assessing students with profound and multiple learning disabilities. These include:

Coupe, J., Barton, M., Collins, L., Levy, D. and Murphy, D. (1985) *The Affective Communication Assessment.* Manchester: Manchester Education Authority.

Dewart, H. and Summers, S. (1988) *The Pragmatics Profile of Early Communication Skills.* Slough: NFER-Nelson.

Kiernan, C. and Reid, B. (1987) The *Pre-verbal Communication Schedule*. Slough: NFER-Nelson.

It is significant that all three schedules have communication as their primary interest, demonstrating the importance of developing social interaction to begin to make sense of the world.

Managing Assessment

Interactive assessment assumes that assessment is a continuous process. There is no need for every session to be monitored and ticked off although a good teacher is aware all the time of the potential of every activity for indicating progress. Again, manageability is a consideration. It has been found that a notebook constantly available is useful for unexpected learning to be recorded but many teachers find that weekly recording is sufficient in most cases (*see* Session 10 for more discussion of recording). Some students may be progressing very quickly or very slowly and the timing of assessment should be adjusted accordingly.

It is also helpful to set up specific activities to provide evidence of learning. This is not meant in the sense of a test or examination, but as a diagnostic tool to inform the next step in learning. For example after some work on memory strategies, it might be helpful to discuss with the students, the need to see how far they can use what they have learned without help. They could then be asked to fetch items from another room whilst being encouraged to articulate their methods of remembering. If appropriate, assistance can then be offered and measured (as discussed above) to inform the next steps of learning.

One of the biggest problems identified by teachers is the practical organisation of time to enable assessment to take place. This can be the product of thinking that teaching and assessment are separate. Once they are seen as part of the same process, the problem of finding time to assess is less important. For example (see overleaf), several teaching sessions can be followed by an assessment opportunity.

Building assessment into teaching in this way ensures that it is a regular and routine occurrence. The exercise described overleaf was specifically set up to provide evidence of learning but the letter itself had validity and learning opportunities still existed for the students.

Assessment of Understanding and the Thinking Process

It is relatively easy to find guidance for assessing the acquisition of skills but it is more difficult to find help with assessing student's understanding or their thinking processes. Assessing understanding implies making judgement. Skills are either demonstrated or they are not but understanding has to be inferred. Collecting evidence is crucial to assessing understanding and this may begin with the gathering of examples of students using individual skills. Sometimes the accumulation of these examples can lead teachers to judge that understanding has been reached. For example understanding of counting could be attributed to students who can consistently count accurately different objects in a variety of circumstances, both when requested and spontaneously displaying knowledge of when counting is appropriate. They must consistently

Example

A group of students had been working on letter writing for several weeks. They had talked about and tried out a variety of different kinds of letters, mainly to friends and relatives. Their teacher wanted to check their progress and plan the next stage of the project. She told the group that she wanted to see what they could do without her help for the first part of the session and then she would give any assistance that was needed to complete the exercise. The letter was to be an invitation to lunch to a friend. There were possibilities for the students to find help from each other, from the dictionary and from displays on the wall. The teacher expected there to be a variety of responses to the task and she decided that her prompt list should contain the following categories:

- letter layout
- envelope layout
- address
  - own address
  - addressee
- signing-off phrase
- clarity of message
- accuracy of English
- awareness of purpose
- assistance found independently
- assistance needed to complete the task

From the notes she made, the teacher was able to plan the next stage of the project which was to move onto more formal letters requesting information. She wanted these to be part of a larger project to plan and run a weekend away, so the context would be very real and have consequences for the group.

obey the rules of counting, which McConkey and McEvoy (1986) lists as:

- Identify the items making up the set.
- Recall the number names in the proper order.
- Give each item in the set one number name.
- Remember the items they have counted and those which remain.
- Realise the last number counted is the total for the set.

Attributing understanding of counting is considerably more complex than just ticking off when the student can count unifix cubes or pictures of rabbits. Attempting to isolate the processes students are using in their thinking is also demanding and the following prompt sheet may be of some help to cue the teacher into aspects of tasks with which learners have difficulties.

National Curriculum Assessment

For teachers who work in school, it is relevant to consider the compatibility of interactive approaches with the demands of National Curriculum Assessment. Generally interactive approaches are consistent with the 1995 Orders and fit well into the new style Programmes of Study. The teacher assessment which accompanies this and provides level descriptions is based on a 'best fit' style. Teachers are expected to look at the level descriptions and decide which best fits individual pupils. The School Curriculum and Assessment Authority (SCAA) specifically discourages teachers from creating tick lists from these descriptions

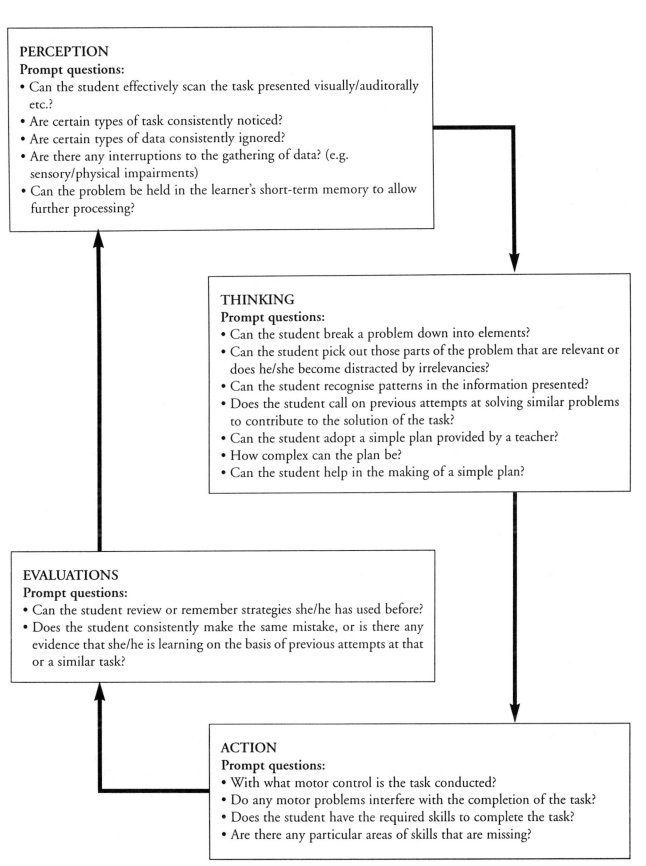

PERCEPTION
Prompt questions:
- Can the student effectively scan the task presented visually/auditorally etc.?
- Are certain types of task consistently noticed?
- Are certain types of data consistently ignored?
- Are there any interruptions to the gathering of data? (e.g. sensory/physical impairments)
- Can the problem be held in the learner's short-term memory to allow further processing?

THINKING
Prompt questions:
- Can the student break a problem down into elements?
- Can the student pick out those parts of the problem that are relevant or does he/she become distracted by irrelevancies?
- Can the student recognise patterns in the information presented?
- Does the student call on previous attempts at solving similar problems to contribute to the solution of the task?
- Can the student adopt a simple plan provided by a teacher?
- How complex can the plan be?
- Can the student help in the making of a simple plan?

EVALUATIONS
Prompt questions:
- Can the student review or remember strategies she/he has used before?
- Does the student consistently make the same mistake, or is there any evidence that she/he is learning on the basis of previous attempts at that or a similar task?

ACTION
Prompt questions:
- With what motor control is the task conducted?
- Do any motor problems interfere with the completion of the task?
- Does the student have the required skills to complete the task?
- Are there any particular areas of skills that are missing?

Figure 6.2 A prompt sheet to form the basis of assessment of the thinking process

as this will not only make more work but will also prevent teachers from viewing pupils in an holistic manner.

Teachers of pupils with learning difficulties can make use of level descriptions to provide prompt sheets for describing the work of pupils who are progressing very slowly through the National Curriculum.

Teachers of students who are not aged between 5 and 16 may wish also to look to parts of the National Curriculum for ideas concerning progression in particular subjects and may find the level descriptions helpful when trying to assess this progress.

2. Reflection

Last Sessions Focus

Begin your reflection by sharing with a partner or with the group an evaluation of the action plan that you made at the end of the previous session. Was it successful? What did you learn? Where might you go next in this area?

This Session's Focus

Discuss the principles of assessment in your school/ college/ centre. You might like to structure your discussion using the following headings:

• Aims of assessment in your workplace.

• Variations for different groups of students.

• Principles that drive your assessment practice.

Your principles might include:

• Students should be involved wherever possible.

• It should not be paper intensive.

• It should aim to give an holistic view of the students.

• Published checklists are used as guidance only, etc.

Now make a list of the assessment practice in your school/ college/ centre. Write down what you actually do, which schedules you use, when you assess, what you assess and how it is presented to other people.

How compatible are your principles and practice? What can the interactive view of assessment presented in this session add to what happens?

3. How To Move On

Choose an area of the curriculum and a group of students and design a prompt sheet that would assist and structure your assessment of student progress. Remember the features of interactive assessment and that the purpose of the prompt sheet is to give structure to a description of what you see and hear. Consider the level of detail needed: too much and the sheet becomes a tick list; too little and much will be missed.

This prompt sheet should be personal to your own situation but it will be helpful to discuss it with colleagues as you form it.

4. Action Plan

Write plan to use the prompt sheet you have devised and be prepared to feed back on its use at the next session.

You might also like to identify one aspect of assessment discussed in this session and write an action plan to implement an initial step within your own work setting, e.g. student ownership, observation, questioning, managing assessment, etc.

Further Reading

Reference	Points of Interest
Barrs, M., Ellis, S., Hester, H. and Thomas, A. (1988) *The Primary Language Record.* London: ILEA	Examples of prompt sheets on reading, writing, speaking and listening
Campione, J. (1989) 'Assisted assessment: A taxonomy of strengths and weaknesses', *Journal of Learning Disabilities,* **22**(3),151-16	Assisted assessment
Feuerstein, R., Rand, Y. and Hoffman, M. (1979) *The Dynamic Assessment of Retarded Performers Learning Potential Assessment Device, Theory Instruments and Techniques.* Baltimore: University Park Press.	Dynamic assessment
Kerry, T. (1982) *Effective Questioning.* London: Macmillan.	Questioning
McConkey, R. and McEvoy, J. (1986) *Count Me In.* Dublin: St Michael's House.	Video course assessing and teaching counting
Norwich, B. (1993) *Reappraising Special Education.* London: Cassell.	Process-based assessment
Rose, R., Ferguson, A., Coles, C., Byers, R. and Banes, D. (1994) *Implementing the Whole Curriculum for Pupils with Learning difficulties.* London: David Fulton.	Records of Achievement
Wolfendale, S. (1993) *Assessing Special Educational Needs.* London: Cassell.	Involving students in assessment

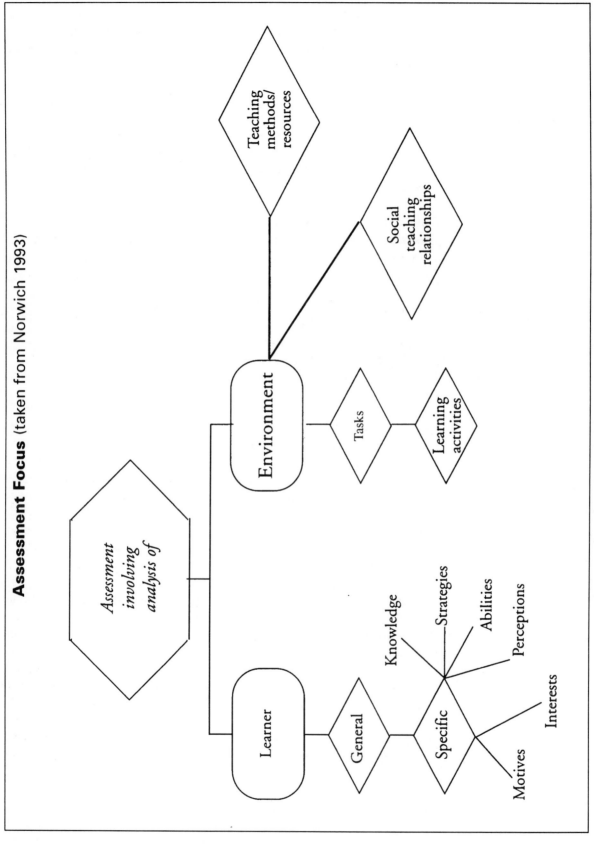

Assessment Focus (taken from Norwich 1993)

Assessment involving analysis of

Learner
- General
- Specific
  - Knowledge
  - Strategies
  - Abilities
  - Perceptions
  - Interests
  - Motives

Environment
- Tasks
- Learning activities
- Teaching methods/resources
- Social teaching relationships

Interactive Approaches to Teaching. © Mark Collis and Penny Lacey

SESSION 7

Creating an Interactive Environment

Although many staff are skilled at providing an attractive environment in their classrooms/ working areas, it may not be that they have considered how to maximise its potential for teaching and learning. Neither might they have considered how they can vary the grouping of learners nor how they might like to organise the available experts. It is very difficult to make the best use of learners' thinking skills in an environment which is preventing them from exercising freedom of choice, learning from mistakes and solving problems.

1. Focus

Physical Environment

At its simplest levee physical environment needs to be organised to make accessible the elements of independent living. For example in a school classroom, pencils, paper, books, scissors, etc. need to be in containers which are available for pupils to help themselves when they have decided what tools they need to complete a task. Sometimes the obvious presence of such things are prompts to encourage choice. In a class where there are a few learners who are likely to damage themselves or others or destroy objects, then access to a cupboard which is only unlocked during supervised work periods may be the answer to providing this independence to other students.

One of the basic tenets of interactive approaches is that learners should be encouraged to be actively engaged in their own learning. It is not enough to be told something, you need to experience it. You can't skip the stage of playing with your food if you are going to learn anything of its properties although you might be able to learn to eat in an acceptable manner. Active learning areas need space, especially when the learners are at an early stage of development. They need space to move about and learn through their own actions, through touching, building, pulling, scrutinising, experimenting. They need to work on their own, in groups, with a friend. They need to work large and work small. The arrangement of this space is important because it affects everything that the learners do.

Moving on a little from equipment and learning areas is the importance of giving opportunities for learning from simple routines like tidying up. It is interesting, at this point, to take an example from the High/Scope classroom.

In the home corner, there are four sizes of saucepan, each with a matching outline on the wall painted in a graded sequence. When the children put away the saucepans they are able to practise matching and see an example of gradation as well as learning the importance of replacing objects after play. The adults can reinforce this through suitable verbal interaction, helping the children to see the relevance of the exercise.

This can be transferred to a teenage or adult situation in entirety if the learners are at the stage of development where they need to practise early matching skills. Alternatively the principle can be adopted and altered to fit learners who are more able. Kitchen drawers can be labelled with pictures, symbols or words and these can be incorporated into simple cards which in turn can be used as prompts for carrying out kitchen routines.

Objects of Reference

For learners at an early stage of development, employing objects to represent activities, places, people and times can be very helpful in attempting to make sense of a world which seems to be unpredictable and frustrating. The RNIB promote the idea of objects of reference for children with visual impairments but there is much in the techniques which is helpful for people with learning difficulties.

At a simple level, the teacher chooses a cup to represent a drink and can help the learner to use it to anticipate a drink arriving. In a more complex situation, a little bell, a piece of rubber mat and a bracelet could all be stuck onto a card. This can then be read as if it was an instruction card: 'You have got music (bell) in the hall (piece of rubber mat) with Jenny (bracelet)'. It can also be used to facilitate recall.

Using objects of reference in this way enables the environment to become really responsive to individual needs. It is not just an attractive display, it is functional and encourages interaction from the learner.

Symbol Timetables

A useful strategy for helping learners who need help with understanding the pattern of the day is to employ a symbol timetable. For some it is appropriate for this to be in some way interactive. For example, learners may need, physically to move cards with symbols representing activities from a store into the correct time slot for the day. They may then be able to refer to this when moving from one activity to another. Using objects of reference in this way can help the learner move towards a more abstract appreciation of time passing.

Working with objects of reference and symbol timetables has been found to be particularly useful with learners with autism who often have great difficulty in making sense of the world around them. Using objects or symbols in this way can offer them the scaffold necessary to encourage the beginnings of understanding which, in turn, can prevent the tantrums which represent the fear and frustration they feel.

A Multi-Sensory Environment

It is necessary to consider the multi-sensory environment on two levels. Firstly, it is worth considering the learning area and its 'sympathy' with the learners. For instance, is the ambient noise level so high that learners with hearing impairments or who have not yet begun to use their hearing effectively, are unable to interact with the most relevant sound source, which might be the teacher talking or a noise-making piece of equipment? This is a remarkably easy trap to fall into. Two people talking, the radio on, adjusting Velcro fasteners on standing frames, shuffling papers, swishing water can all be potentially distracting sounds when trying to concentrate on something specific. It is impossible to reduce the noise to nothing, especially in an active learning area, but teachers could be more aware of ways of avoiding the problems.

The other aspect of a multi-sensory environment is that of getting the best out of multi-sensory rooms. There is enormous teaching and learning potential in the wealth of equipment currently available. However, trips into the multi-sensory room need careful planning and precise evaluation if the potential is to be realised.

An important use of this kind of environment is to set it up to be as interactive as possible through the use of switches operated in a variety of ways. At a very simple level this enables learners to develop understanding of cause and effect and, at a more sophisticated level, they can move towards independence by turning on the radio or TV, opening the door or moving an electric wheelchair.

Offering control to learners is an important aspect of interactive approaches to learning. It is often easier and quicker for teachers to do things for students and it is safer to keep switches for expensive equipment out of reach. Relinquishing some of our control is undeniably risky but it is essential if children and adults with learning difficulties are to live an ordinary life as far as possible. Ordinary people have likes and dislikes, they repeat activities they like and avoid those they don't.

Group Work

Although many of the activities suitable for learners with profound disabilities will be individually tailored and will, on the whole, take place when there is one teacher working with one learner, there are many occasions when students with learning difficulties can work together in a group situation. The social exchange encouraged through group work can be a powerful learning tool. Psychologists such as Bruner or Vygotsky placed great emphasis on the importance of social interaction on the learning process.

The influence of behaviourism has been such that individual work has been seen as the only effective way of teaching students who have difficulties in learning. Working in groups has only recently been considered suitable or within their abilities. There are several different ways of organising this depending upon the task selected and the social ability of the students involved.

The simplest form of group work is suitable for learners at an early stage of communication. It involves the teacher with three or four students round him or her and each takes turns to receive individual attention. The engagement should be fairly short and repeated often so that no one is left unstimulated for long and yet can be given short 'switch off' times as part of the activity and plenty of opportunities to anticipate when their turn is about to begin. This configuration might be suitable for simple cookery which involves different steps or for a drama game which involves turns to fit a rhyme.

Strictly this not really group work, it is only grouping the students to be engaged in parallel activities. When the students are more aware of each other and of the different steps in an activity and how they can fit together to produce a whole, then 'jigsawing' may be a possibility.

For instance, again in cookery, students can be responsible for different stages of the meal so that working together means that the meal is ready at the correct time. Creating a piece of artwork can be done in this way as well. Each person does a different job as part of the whole and the finished article is the result of one person cutting, another placing and a third sticking. It encourages them to notice each other and begin to understand what is meant by co-operation.

During jigsawing, some thought should be given to the waiting time inevitable in sharing tasks. If students are likely to get restless whilst watching others at work, then it might be necessary to organise the session in a slightly different way. For instance all students could be involved in their own stage separately and are only brought together at the end. This can be a good introduction to the idea of sharing tasks.

The zenith of group work is genuine problem solving, where there is room for interpretation and initiative, sharing ideas and trying them out to see what happens. This can begin simply with partners working out that tables are needed for an activity which they must carry together to the place in which they are wanted. Later problems can be much more taxing and can contain several different stages where it is only possible to solve them if students work together. Producing a group newspaper is a common example of encouraging co-operation and interdependence especially if there is one person responsible for illustrations, one for layout, another for news etc.

Teachers of students with learning difficulties are often faced with a group having a wide variety of abilities which can challenge the concept of group work. It appears to be impossible to find anything in common between the members. In this case it is possible to have a basic plan for all, the detail of which is differentiated to fit the needs of each student.

For example, 'Going on a Picnic' could be organised in this way. The more able students could be responsible for planning and making lists of equipment which less able peers could find and assemble. Making sandwiches and drinks can be divided in a similar manner, depending upon ability. Some individual objectives could be independent of the actual activity. For example, a learner at an early stage of development may be working on eye contact, tracking and simple grasp but these can be built into what the rest of the group are doing.

Many teachers find it difficult to include group members who have profound and multiple disabilities, but in fact their needs are so basic that they can be included in almost any activity. Often time has to be given and a quiet moment found but once the group gets used to stopping and waiting for their less able peers, it becomes a routine.

This level of differentiation is not possible for all activities, especially those which are more academic in their nature, although it may be possible to be working on tracking skills whilst moving an historical artefact across the visual field of a student with PMLD. It could not, however, be argued that this is a history lesson for these students!

Group work is not the answer to every activity but it is another tool to use and it encourages the development of a different set of skills from those employed in individual work. Sharing, waiting, helping and advising are all used and it is an ideal situation in which to encourage spontaneous communication and problem solving skills. Mixed ability groups are particularly effective for providing good learning models for the less able members of the group as well as encouraging the more able members to take greater responsibility.

Staff Teamwork

The way in which staff view their roles is of central importance in creating an interactive environment. Some of this has been covered in Sessions 2 and 3 but one aspect which has not is that of management. How can the staff who work in the classroom be organised? Who is responsible for that organisation? How important is it to be clear about people's different roles?

It seems of prime importance that everyone who is available to work in the classroom should be considered part of a team. To meet the diverse needs of the students, this team should be encouraged to work in a collaborative manner. Collaboration can be characterised by the extent to which team members share their expertise with each other. Although each person will have a specific role for which they were primarily employed, such as teacher, nursery nurse, occupational therapist, support worker, etc., the actual work that is carried out with the students is likely to be overlapping. Team members must spend time training each other so that students receive integrated care and education. It is very easy for fragmentation to occur as teachers concentrate on academic work, assistants work mainly on social skills and therapists only concern themselves with their particular specialisms. Students with learning difficulties will find learning much easier if their needs are addressed in an holistic manner. If everyone knows the concepts that are central or the words that are being added to the vocabulary then there can be maximum opportunities for practice.

Working as a genuinely collaborative team is not easy. Although it is not necessary for everyone in the team to be equal, it is desirable that everyone should be equally valued. Planning should be carried out together as much as possible because full collaboration is not achieved by one person making all the decisions and telling the others what to do. Conversely, not every decision needs to be made by all team members. Trusting each other is an important part of teamwork. Working collaboratively implies finding the time to talk together as a team. Members need to get to know one another, share expertise and solve problems together. They need time to work out a common set of records and co-ordinate assessments and they need time to plan. Management support is of paramount importance so that there is flexibility built into timetables. The need for time for discussion lessens as the team gets more practice at working together but *teams cannot function without time to talk.*

2. Reflection

Last Session's Focus

Begin your reflection by sharing with a partner or with the group an evaluation of the action plan that you made at the end of the previous session. Was it successful? What did you learn? Where might you go next in this area?

This Session's Focus

Here are six statements concerning the creation of an interactive environment:

1. Classroom displays have ongoing learning possibilities.
2. Students can be involved in organising their own learning environment.
3. Careful use of multi-sensory rooms can encourage independence.
4. Group work is not only possible but desirable for mixed ability classes.
5. Interaction between staff and students involves giving control to students.
6. Collaborative teamwork provides opportunities for staff development.

(a) Take each statement and discuss it with a partner or within your small group. Begin by expressing your understanding of the statement and whether you agree with it. Be sure to give your reasons for agreeing or disagreeing. If you disagree, adjust the statement until it expresses something with which you do agree.

(b) Divide a piece of flip chart paper into six and provide one example for each statement, showing how it can be achieved.

(c) Share with the whole group.

3. How To Move On

Choose one of the following areas on which to concentrate your development:

1. The physical environment.
2. Group work.
3. Staff teamwork.

Divide a piece of paper into two and list your strengths and weaknesses in this area. Discuss these with a partner.

4. Action Plan

Take one of the weaknesses which can be tackled in the intervening time between this session and the next and write an action plan to enable its achievement or partial achievement.

You might have chosen the physical environment and the need for providing more learning experiences through the arrangement of equipment. Your action plan might look like this:

1. Label three boxes with the symbols for biscuits, crisps and fruit to use for snack time.
2. Help the students to fill the boxes with appropriate food.
3. Let them choose what they want at snack time from the symbols.

4. For more able students, sometimes sabotage the boxes and symbols so that the task is more difficult or encourage them to negotiate with each other when there is not enough to go round.

This may be one small idea but it can be the beginning of more perhaps for labelling containers for scissors and hammers and paper of different sizes which can be available when choosing them or putting them away.

Share your action plan with your partner and be prepared to report back briefly at the beginning of the next session.

Further Reading	*Reference*	*Points of Interest*
	Hohmann, M., Banet, B. and Weikhart, D. (1979) *Young Children in Action*. Yipsilanti: High/Scope Press.	High/Scope classroom
	Lacey, P. and Lomas, J. (1993) *Support Services and the Curriculum: A Practical Guide to Collaboration*. London: David Fulton Publishers.	Staff Teamwork
	NCC (1993) *The National Curriculum for Children with Severe Learning Difficulties*. York: NCC.	Symbol timetables
	Ockleford, A. (1994) *Objects of Reference: Promoting Communication Skills and Concept Development with Visually Impaired Children who have other Disabilities*. London: RNIB.	Objects of Reference
	Rose,R. (1991) 'A jigsaw approach to group work,' *British Journal of Special Education*, 18(2), 54-7.	Groupwork

An Interactive Environment

1. Classroom displays have ongoing learning possibilities.

2. Students can be involved in organising their own learning environment.

3. Careful use of multi-sensory rooms can encourage independence.

4. Group work is not only possible but desirable for mixed ability classes.

5. Interaction between staff and students involves giving control to students.

6. Collaborative teamwork provides opportunities for staff development.

Interactive Approaches to Teaching. © Mark Collis and Penny Lacey

SESSION 8

Planning Aims and Objectives

This session is concerned with long- and short-term curriculum planning.
Different kinds of objectives are discussed and suggestions are made for how
these can be the basis of students' individual educational programmes.

1. Focus

Different Kinds of Objectives

Writing programmes of work for students with learning difficulties includes
ensuring that individual needs are clearly identified so that precise objectives
can be devised. The amount of precision depends on the approach adopted for
the area of work under consideration. For instance, task-orientated work such
as teeth cleaning and counting by rote lend themselves to a traditionally
expressed behavioural objective such as:

> On the request, 'count these (objects)', N. verbally counts (objects) from **1**
> **to 10** with fluency and without mistakes on three consecutive occasions.

The result of this objective is instant recall of the words which stand for
numbers in the order in which we say them whilst pointing to each object once.
Success can be indicated through a simple tick or cross. However it tells us
nothing of the understanding that this student has of counting. It is necessary
to add objectives expressed in a different manner to be sure that progress in
comprehension can be demonstrated. This kind of objective will be more open-
ended and there will be space for a record of what happened. The objective
might look like this:

> N. counts objects, people, pictures etc. (no more than 10) to ensure that I
> there are enough for the task in hand (e.g. enough drinks for each person
> to have one). (Record several instances of situations when you judge N. is
> demonstrating understanding of the purpose of counting.)

The result of this objective is examples of the ways in which this particular student was using counting purposefully. Success is indicated through short comments culminating in a judgement made by the teacher. It would be expected that the way in which the counting was demonstrated was as important as the result of the counting (i.e. that everyone had a drink). This may even appear in the objective:

> N. is reminded to think of the strategy she is going to use to count objects (no more than 10). She indicates what strategy she will use and counts the objects accurately. (The strategy adopted may be to push or place each object to one side after it has been counted but record any strategy used.)

The result of this objective is evidence that N. has adopted a strategy to help her to understand that she must count each object once only. She still needs reminding and the teacher is providing the appropriate scaffolding to enable this basic understanding to develop. The suggestion of a possible strategy within the objective indicates previous teaching where this was demonstrated but there is still room for demonstration of other equally effective ways of ensuring accurate counting should this occur. Lots of possibilities for practising this should be provided in relevant contexts so that the strategy is generalised. Games are particularly useful for providing many opportunities for counting in the same way over and over again. These will mostly have to be home-made to provide the control over the numbers and the simplicity that will be needed by many students.

Relating to the National Curriculum

Writing objectives in this manner relates directly to the Programmes of Study of the revised National Curriculum which is relevant for teachers working in schools. The Programme of Study for Mathematics Key Stage 1 Number includes the words:

'Pupils should be taught to:

count orally up to 10..., knowing the number names; count collections of objects, checking the total; ...'

In the previous section, we have basically taken this PoS and suggested possible components for students with learning difficulties. This has revealed the complexity of learning to count effectively and understanding what this really means. It is very tempting to rely on a simple behavioural objective and think that students have achieved counting when it can be ticked off on a checklist. This is patently not sufficient and different kinds of objectives can enable the various aspects of counting to be covered.

Open-ended Objectives

There are times when completely open-ended objectives are useful, especially when encouraging problem solving capabilities.

This kind of objective contains within it enough information for the situation to be set up and to provide for the support that the student will need to solve the problem. Records will show how the problem was tackled and

Example

N. is presented with a situation where two friends have been invited to lunch and there is not enough to eat. There is sufficient time to buy something extra or cook something from the store cupboard. The teacher asks pertinent questions to enable her to work out her plan of action, e.g. 'What have we got in the cupboard?' or 'How much money have we got?' 'What will you have to do first?' Record with N:

(a) Her action plan and what happened.

(b) What kind of support she needed, including examples of questions used.

(c) What she achieved on her own.

(d) What she needs to do next time.

where the student needs to improve. By definition the end product is not specified but of course in practice teachers will have several ideas about how the problem will be solved.

A similarly open-ended objective is needed for experiential activities. An example might be:

Group A will be presented with modelling clay, rolling pins and pieces of fabric along with a variety of implements to cut and shape the materials. They will be encouraged to explore the materials in different ways. (Any models will be preserved but the object is not necessarily to produce one.)

The results of this objective will be many and various and anything can be accepted as legitimate (within the bounds of safety). Records might include a description of the techniques used, or a photograph of what was produced, or the communication demonstrated, or merely the fact that the experience was offered and whether there had been any expression of enjoyment. What is important to capture is the quality of the experience.

There are times when this kind of experience can be used to contain a more precise objective for individual students. For instance, for a student with profound disabilities, during this session with the clay, you might be looking for the following:

X. participates in a simple turn-taking game, passing materials back and forth with another person.

This will result in the materials provided being used as a focus for a simple interactive game designed to encourage social communication. Records will include:

• What happened.

• How far the student was engaged in the game.

• Whether eye contact was achieved.

• If the teacher was able to interpret the student's feelings.

Objectives for Groups

Often, when actually working in the classroom, although there is a plan for the whole group, within that plan there are individual objectives for different students. The group objective might be:

> Students will plan, purchase, prepare, eat and clear up a simple meal. This will be fulfiled over 2 days and will include opportunities for using writing and number skills as well as practical shopping and cooking. All group members will be engaged at a level suitable for their skills and understanding.

There may be other instructions, making the detail of this activity more explicit.

For each individual student, there will be a detailed set of objectives, some of which may be shared with others in the group. The following is an example of individual objectives for a group of eight young people with a variety of learning difficulties.

> John will use the concept keyboard to write his personal shopping list containing things he is allowed for his special diet.
>
> Mary will act as a scribe for the shopping list for the rest of the group using the 'look, cover, write, check' technique.
>
> Mahesh will eye point to the symbols for food to go on the shopping list. Target symbols are bread, butter, apples and cake.
>
> Liz will give the correct money in the supermarket from a selection in her purse (all coins).
>
> Mark will select the correct amount of unbruised fruit for everyone in the group.
>
> Jane will remain part of the group whilst out shopping. (She can take charge of the trolley.)
>
> Peter will demonstrate basic knowledge of hygiene in the kitchen by washing his hands, wearing an apron and, with reminders, keeping his hands away from his face.
>
> Alim will divide suitable food in half or two equal portions when appropriate.

These individual objectives may have to be written in greater detail, especially if staff are unfamiliar with students. However, the principle of using a group activity to contain individual objectives is illustrated. Manageability is a concern when writing objectives for groups of students and obviously it is easier if those with similar needs are grouped together. We are not advocating streaming learners but it is helpful to employ judicious setting .

Contexts

One of the most important elements of an interactive objective is the context in which it is planned and carried out. Behaviourist objectives are often associated with test-like contexts that are controllable so that behaviour can be measured accurately. Interactive objectives are based on different premises which enables a more open-ended approach to measurement. Contexts are deliberately varied, although systematically planned, and they may be unpredictable in terms of people, places, times and settings so that learners can demonstrate what they can do in the real world which in turn can indicate their level of understanding.

It is sometimes helpful to begin teaching a new skill in a controlled context so that the principles are learned with few distractions but if variety is not offered very quickly, the skill may become so strongly associated with one context that it will not be generalised. Higher order understanding cannot be confined to specific contexts.

Although it is possible to plan some contexts within objectives, there will be many occasions when students will achieve success which is not planned. Teaching and record keeping should be sufficiently flexible to enable this to happen. Over-reliance on predetermined objectives can discourage teachers from looking at the learning that is going on in front of them and encourage them only to look for what they think should be happening. There is often a startling difference between what teachers think students are learning and what they actually are. The teacher thinks the student is learning how to count objects when in fact she is learning that the objects she is counting will all fit into the box if she twists every other one through ninety degrees, a valuable lesson in understanding shapes and simple tessellation. Alternatively she may be learning that if she makes certain sounds whilst pointing at objects she will finish quickly and be allowed to do something very much more interesting.

Criteria for Success

Behavioural objectives have very precise criteria for measuring success, spelling out exactly what the student has to do, in what circumstances and how many times. Objectives associated with interactive approaches do not usually specify these in advance with such precision. It is left more open-ended for teachers to judge what they see happening in front of them. The same principles, however, do apply. For instance if we return to counting, teachers would expect to see evidence of understanding counting on several different occasions, using different equipment in different contexts. They would be expected to use their professional judgement to decide how many times would be sensible to expect this evidence of each individual student. This little section concerning criteria can be related to discussions in both the Assessment and Curriculum Sessions concerning how you actually write your curriculum and how you assess students' progress. You might like to consider these three altogether.

Zone of Next Development

Another important element of planning suitable objectives is the precise matching of teaching to learning needs. The psychologist Vygotsky suggested that it is very important to find the zone in the student's development where learning is just beginning so that teaching can be offered where there is both motivation and specific cognitive movement.

Teachers need to become very skilled at observing students to discover that zone of next development. Facilitating open-ended situations can reveal levels of functioning which in turn can give an indication of understanding. Functioning and understanding are by no means synonymous, especially when considering students with learning difficulties and additional disabilities. Poor physical function, for instance, may mask greater understanding and vice versa. In addition, learning may be taking place in one aspect of the student's development which distracts him from responding to teaching in another area which has been observed as potential for development. Normally developing infants find it difficult to increase their vocabulary when they are going through the most demanding stage of learning to walk. Temporarily, language development takes second place while upright balance is mastered sufficiently for it to become automatic. It is like learning to drive. Learners find it difficult to concentrate on learning road signs until control of the car is automatic.

Teachers need to know students extremely well to be able to identify where learning is beginning. There are so many variables. Working closely with parents and other significant carers is of vital importance. Parents and carers usually have a more relaxed and open-ended agenda and can be extremely accurate in summing up the zone of next development. Writing educational objectives together with parents or carers not only increases their accuracy but is the basis for both parties to be striving towards the same goals in the two different contexts. This will increase the possibility of learning taking place.

There are a few published questionnaires which are helpful for interviewing parents and carers to establish their perceptions of where teaching should be placed. Dewart and Summers (1988) is one such and is useful for establishing the abilities and the needs of students who are at a pre-verbal stage of language development. The principles of using a structured interview schedule can be used in other ways to enable teachers to become skilled interviewers, collecting data to inform the writing of educational objectives.

Other Professionals

Parents and carers have invaluable general perceptions of their charges but other professionals have equally valuable knowledge concerning the different abilities and disabilities of students with learning difficulties and experience of effective ways to encourage learning. In the case of a student with multiple disabilities, there may be a large number of professionals involved who between them hold keys to unlocking learning potential which are not available to each individual.

Bringing together this expertise when writing objectives can be of vital importance if maximum learning is to take place. It is usual for each professional to write his or her objectives for the student individually and either work on them separately or expect the teacher at school, college or centre and parents or carers at home to combine them to create a sensible programme for the student. It is becoming recognised that if all professionals, parents and carers plan together then the programme will be more comprehensive and relate directly to the needs of the whole student in an integrated manner. However, writing joint objectives is not easy and professionals and families must be prepared to find the time to gather together, discuss needs and agree priorities before the objectives can be written. Often the actual writing is left to one or two people who then seek agreement from the others.

Sometimes different members of this team have different priorities for the student. When this happens, negotiation is a very useful tool. Some objectives may have to wait for a while, perhaps until more fundamental ones are being worked on or because the student cannot be learning in lots of different areas. Members of the therapy team at the Wolfsen Centre in London talk about 'jostling' and 'queuing' with their objectives. This is not an aggressive activity but the occupational therapist must wait her turn for hand function to become of greatest importance while the physiotherapist works on positioning in general. The speech therapist is on the sidelines waiting to establish what aids are necessary to encourage communication.

Long- and Short-Term Planning

Even though many of the activities associated with interactive approaches are open-ended and outcomes can be surprising, there is still a need to plan in detail. Teachers in one school for children with severe learning difficulties were heard to say, 'We don't have individual programmes for the children any more, we do interactive approaches'. There is a basic misunderstanding in this statement. Advocates of interactive approaches do not suggest that students are offered unplanned activities to 'see what will happen'. Teachers need to look very carefully at the current level of development of each learner so that the activities offered can be closely matched to the next steps. They must also be sufficiently open-minded to accept whatever learning take place and build on that in future activities. It might also be helpful to consider that there are some objectives, particularly for students with profound disabilities, that are designed to set a direction for development and may not actually be fully attainable independently.

It is important to plan both in the long and the short term, the first in general and the second in detail. Long-term plans can always be adjusted in the light of actual learning but it is important to take this wider view. A long-term aim might be:

> to work out and understand how to balance a simple weekly budget for snacks

and a short-term plan in the middle might be:

> Sam will add up the amount spent on snacks each day using a calculator. The teacher will give verbal prompts at each step trying general questions first, e.g. 'which button next?'. Please record exactly the amount of help Sam requires and the understanding you feel he has reached .

For most teachers of students with learning difficulties, the aims and objectives outlined in this session seem familiar. Certainly, the need for careful planning has been a feature of this branch of education since the beginning of the 1980s. Planning interactive objectives is merely an extension of this, encouraging teachers to have a broader view of what constitutes an objective and to look more widely at what their students should be learning.

2. Reflection

Bring your planning sheets to the discussion session and with a partner or in a small group, analyse the way in which you write your objectives in the light of the above focus. Look particularly for opportunities for students to:

1. Explore the world around them.

2. Take control of their lives and learning.

3. Learn from making mistakes.

4. Demonstrate their understanding of the world around them.

5. Use strategies to improve their learning in general.

6. Learn from social interaction.

7. Solve problems.

8. Take responsibility.

9. Negotiate their own learning.

10. Achieve independence.

Some of these feature in the focus for this session but others have been discussed in earlier sessions so you may need to remind yourself about them during your discussion.

3. How To Move On

Discuss with your partner or group where you need to make changes and additions to cover the ten areas suggested.

Choose two of these and together write some examples which refer to the students with whom you work.

4. Action Plan

Try out these examples to gauge their effectiveness in directing your work during the time between this and the next session. Evaluate in terms of:

1. How well they cover the interactive activities you offer to the students.

2. How helpful they were at directing activity sessions.

3. How easy they were to follow by other members of the team.

4. How well they lent themselves to record keeping.

Further Reading	*Reference*	*Points of Interest*
	Byers, R. (1990) 'Topics: From myths to objectives', *British Journal of Special Education*, **17(3)**,109–112.	Placing individual objectives within group sessions
	Dewart, H. and Summers, S. (1988) *The Pragmatics Profile of Early Communication Skills.* Slough: NFER Nelson.	Schedule for interviewing parents and carers
	Brennan, W. (1985) *Curriculum for Special Education.* Milton Keynes: Open University Press.	Writing different kinds of objectives
	School Curriculum and Assessment Authority (1996) *Planning the Curriculum for Pupils with Profound and Multiple Learning Difficulties.* London: SCAA.	
	Sebba, J., Byers, R. and Rose, R. (1993) *Redefining the Whole Curriculum for Pupils with Learning Difficulties.* London: David Fulton Publishers.	Long- and short-term planning
	National Curriculum Council (1993) *The National Curriculum and Pupils with Severe Learning Difficulties.* York: NCC.	Planning within the National Curriculum

How do your objectives enable students to:

1. Explore the world around them.

2. Take control of their lives and learning.

3. Learn from making mistakes.

4. Demonstrate their understanding of the world around them.

5. Use strategies to improve their learning in general.

6. Learn from social interaction.

7. Solve problems.

8. Take responsibility.

9. Negotiate their own learning.

10. Achieve independence?

Interactive Approaches to Teaching. © Mark Collis and Penny Lacey

SESSION 9

Curriculum Design and Development

In this session we propose that teachers, faced with the onerous task of curriculum design, should consider the principles that will determine the design and focus of their curriculum, particularly in the light of interactive approaches.

1. Focus

Background

Traditionally the formal curriculum for students with learning difficulties has been based on an assessment of skills which has resulted in hierarchies of precise behavioural objectives. We have suggested several times in this text that this precision has been of great benefit to schools and colleges and the following list sums up these benefits in terms of curriculum design.

- It has provided a much needed structure for teaching and a theoretical background that can be used to justify what is done on a daily basis.
- It has enabled the whole concept of targeted learning, which encourages teachers to be precise about what exact learning is expected to result from their efforts.
- This in turn enables the outcomes to be easily assessed against clear objectives.
- The result has been that teaching programmes have pinpointed certain learning outcomes.

For 10–15 years this has been the dominant curriculum structure in the learning difficulties field and most schools and colleges have documents which reflect it.

However, over the years, many teachers have developed a wider view of the curriculum so that for them, a structure based on behavioural principles has been restrictive. An interactive model provides them with opportunities to include what has become classroom practice, but which has not really been reflected within the written documents.

> An interactive perspective to curriculum design is distinct in that it should enable the student to:
>
> Be active.
> - *Take* control.
> - *Learn* through the development of communication and sociability.
> - *Learn* through the development of thinking processes.

Thus, these are aspects of learning which must be added to the traditional curriculum. We are not suggesting that skills-based precision should be thrown out, only that an interactive perspective should be added.

In designing such a curriculum it may be worthwhile first asking the following questions:

> - How can it demonstrate progress on a variety of learning dimensions (e.g. understanding, knowledge, skills, creativity, experiential learning), without becoming unmanageable?
> - How can it be sufficiently flexible to enable the teacher and learner to negotiate a path through what is to be learned and the learning methods needed?
> - How can it be flexible enough to be responsive to the range of individual learning needs presented by all the students within the school or centre?
> - How does it provide recognition of the value of the process as well as the product of learning?
> - How far can it recognise the integrated nature of the curriculum?

Answers to these questions are not simple and reflect the complexity of providing a framework which covers all the learning needs of students with learning difficulties.

Following this brief introduction, we will now try to provide a more detailed rationale for including interactive perspectives in curriculum design.

What does an interactive approach to curriculum design offer?

For the teacher

An interactive style curriculum:

- *Can enable and foster a breadth of teaching styles* – The style that teachers adopt is not rigidly prescribed. Instead they are encouraged to match the teaching style that best suits the learning need. For example, teaching the putting on of a sock may well best be achieved through a behavioural backward-chaining technique, whilst making a hot drink may be better tackled in a problem solving manner.

- *Values the professional decisions/judgements of the teacher* – The curriculum should provide a structure without limiting or constraining what is taught. Teachers should not be limited to teaching what comes next on a checklist of skills. Their professional opinions and intuitions are crucial to the successful design of the learning situation. The curriculum should not simply provide a structure into which the learner is 'plugged', rather it becomes a tool for the teacher to select from and use in programme planning. The curriculum should be seen as the servant rather than as the master.

- *Can effectively complement the structure provided by the National Curriculum* – Words such as 'explore', 'experience' and 'investigate' used in the National Curriculum Revised Orders (1995) suggest the learner must be active in the learning process. There has in the past been almost a fear of the inclusion of such terminology into educational objectives driven by a skills model because of its imprecision but the effect of this has been to constrain *what* is taught and *how* it is taught.

- *Does not restrict the teacher simply to the teaching of skills* – An interactive curriculum not only places importance on the teaching of knowledge and understanding but also for example, on the fostering of creativity and imagination. In short, it implies a wide conception of what teaching and learning are about.

- *Is a logical next phase in curriculum management terms* – Many schools with an objectives/ behaviourally based curriculum can move logically onto this wider conception of curriculum. The transition that is required does not necessarily mean the abandonment of all previous work. Rather it can add to the existing skills based curriculum framework in a way that moves teaching and learning forward – but not just changing because it represents a fashionable new theory!

For the learner

An interactive curriculum:

- *Is a student centred curriculum* in that learners have opportunities to exert some control over it. They can determine a certain amount of what is learnt and how it is learnt. They are not simply plugged into it. An interactive curriculum should be dependent on the response of the learner and cannot stand alone.

  The curriculum must, at the same time, provide a structure or framework for teaching. It should provide opportunities to demonstrate progression without constraining the path through what is learnt. It should allow for things to happen that are unplanned.

- *Enables opportunities for understanding* – Students need to understand how the world works and how they can influence what goes on around them. They can be taught mechanistically how to put on their coats but they also need to understand about feeling cold, about the weather, about getting wet and about when it is appropriate to put on and take off a coat.

- *Is intrinsically motivating* – If the task is sufficiently motivating, there should be no need to attach artificial rewards to the process of learning. Completing tasks for sweets or tokens can encourage the learner to focus on the reward rather than on the task and its purpose. Motivation for individual students should be considered by teachers so that it can be built into the task and not bolted on.

- *Enable them to learn to learn* – It may be argued that *what* is learned is of secondary significance to the development of the ability to learn, so that when confronted with problems in real life the individual has more highly developed learning and problem solving strategies. The curriculum becomes merely a vehicle by which these wider strategies are learnt. The learner becomes increasingly reflexive and responsive to adapt to different day-to-day situations. In this way we return to the importance of independence through the conferring of control.

How might the move be made to a more interactive curriculum?

Curriculum development should result from a process of evaluation of the existing curriculum – how the curriculum has been shown to meet the educational needs of the learners.

Staff may like to ask the questions given in Table 9.1.

Phases of development	Key questions
Where are we now?	What is the existing curriculum structure? Does it enable or obstruct learning? Does it enable the sort of learning we wish to encourage? How has it proven to be successful? What are its failings?
Where do we want to be?	What are the educational principles we hold dear?
How will we get there?	How can we incorporate these principles into our curriculum design? Do we want to adapt the existing structure to meet the requirements of these principles?
What do we want to do?	What is the school's vision? Precisely what changes to curriculum design do we want to make? What are its priorities for development? What actually is possible?

Table 9.1 Adapted from Ainscow *et al.*(1994).

Models of Curriculum Design

The following models are offered as examples of the attempts of different schools to employ some of the principles of interactive approaches. They are not in any way meant to be prescriptive but are offered to encourage discussion. Although we have only given examples from school settings, the principles embodied in them can be applied to any teaching and learning context.

Example 1: Early mathematics at School A

School A. found that although skills were well documented in their curriculum, understanding, knowledge and attitudes were not. They decided to leave the skills curriculum as it was and to add a structure for encouraging the development of pupils' understanding, knowledge and attitudes. They began with understanding for which they devised prompt sheets containing what might constitute demonstration of understanding. This is one example from the early mathematics curriculum.

Discrimination

Observe the level of understanding demonstrated by the child in natural situations. Record exactly what you judge to be the level of understanding of the concept of 'odd one out' or 'different'. Be specific with objects, circumstances, language, limitations. You will need several different examples as evidence.

Suspected areas:

(a) shows understanding of same and difference in the natural making of sets during play.

(b) points out things that are different in normal conversation.

(c) points out differences in areas such as feel, speed, sound, size etc.

(d) plays discrimination games with picture cards.

(e) finds the odd one out in a freely bag.

(f) can interchange words such as 'different', 'not the same', 'odd,' 'not like'.

Example 2: A milestones model at School B

After much within-school discussion it was felt that milestones would provide the teacher with opportunities to demonstrate progress, without completely pre-determining the path of learning that any one child might take. The milestone may describe any piece of learning, whether that be an understanding gained, creativity shown, or a skill gained. Characteristically, milestones do not provide an exhaustive list, but rather offer descriptions of sample behaviours/understandings or knowledge gained. The list does not provide a rigid structure, and takes into account that many students will not progress in a standard way through a developmental scheme. The curriculum is designed so that the student can move through the material in a flexible manner. Associated with each milestone is a series of activity ideas, which are designed to act as prompts to the teacher, to inspire their thinking.

The following is an example.

English: Speaking and listening

(via) Listening

Milestones	Example activities
1. Shows clear evidence of enjoyment of music	Use instruments that are easy to hold or that are strapped on. Hang bell within reach
9. Looks at pictures while adult talks about them	Use large, bright pictures or big books

A common structure throughout curriculum documents was thought to be useful but in practice all subjects did not lend themselves to the same format. The result was that slightly different structures were adopted, although there was care to adhere to the educational principles that had been established at the outset.

Example 3: Mathematics levels at School C.

School C decided to introduce their own levels which cut across the National Curriculum levels and are presented in similar ways to the programmes of study, defining areas to be taught. They provide greater detail for the early stages of the National Curriculum using a similar

language. This example is again from the Mathematics curriculum.

Number

Level A:

- Relationships: one-to-one, one-to-many, many-to-one.
- Responding to materials providing multi-sensory stimulation.
- Sorting things that go together – colours, sizes, shapes.
- Early discrimination: handling familiar and unfamiliar objects having a range of tactile qualities, sizes, etc.

Level B:

- Relationships: one-to-one, one-to-many, many-to-one.
- Sorting things that go together – colours, sizes, shapes.
- Matching colours.
- Counting 'one', use of number, rhymes.
- Playing shop – concept of exchange.

Level C:

- Relationships: one-to-one, one-to-many, many-to-one.
- Sorting things that go together – colours, sizes, shapes.
- Comparing sets for equivalence.
- Matching colours, size, shapes 1-5.
- Counting – matching numeral to set.
- Ordering – first and last.
- Conservation of number.
- Playing shop – coin recognition.

There are six levels altogether, taking pupils through to understanding number value 100+ and place value.

An Integrated Interactive curriculum

Although it may be necessary to document the curriculum divided into subjects, it is perfectly possible for students to experience it through an integrated system. The most common way to manage this is through topic work. Until the 1990s it was quite difficult to find topic work in schools and colleges for students with learning difficulties. Most lessons were precisely directed towards specific skill acquisition. If topic work was observed it was mainly to bind together Humanities or the Creative Arts and it happened in the afternoons when 'serious' learning has already taken place in the morning.

Topic work has more potential than that and this has now become recognised. However, there have been many criticisms of the way in which topics are run. HMI have been very scathing, writing of poorly conceived topics where students copy mindlessly from books and learn little. Clear planning and careful organisation can prevent this from happening and encourage very effective interactive learning opportunities.

Example 4: Cognition at Rectory Paddock School

Rectory Paddock School published *In Search of a Curriculum* in the 1980s but despite being more than 10 years old, their documented attempts at providing a curriculum for 'Memory, Metamemory and Executive Control' are useful to consider, especially as few school's curriculum documents include much detail in this area of learning. This is an extract from Part 1 – Memory Strategies:

Auditory-vocal Rehearsal

5. The child is asked to repeat a short sequence of one-syllable words immediately after hearing them. The task is then made progressively more demanding by the teacher varying the length and number of words.

6. The child is asked to fetch a number of (named) groceries from a table.

7. The child takes a message from one member of staff to another. The task is made more demanding by increasing the distance between them, interposing distractions (e.g. door to be opened) and lengthening the message.

8. (Rehearsal with Organisation) The child is asked to remember a six- figure telephone number.

This curriculum is supported by an Executive Control Task record sheet with a prompt list to assist record keeping. The suggested areas for assessment are:

1. Teacher sets task.

2. Child assesses difficulty.

3. Child considers possible strategies.

4. Child chooses or does not choose strategy.

5. Child carries out task (with or without strategy).

6. Child assesses own performance.

7. Teacher provides feedback.

8. If success – reinforcement; if failure – child chooses new (or same) strategy/reviews strategies/re-assesses difficulty.

Seven stages of a topic (Taken from Lacey, P. and Lomas, J. (1993) *Support Services and the Curriculum.* David Fulton Publishers.)

Stage 1 – Brainstorm ideas using a topic web and decide what kind of things should be offered to be learned (include students where possible and as many relevant members of staff as are available).

Stage 2 – Relate these ideas to the whole curriculum (including the National Curriculum for schools) to ensure breadth and balance over the year.

Stage 3 – Consult with everyone who is involved with the students, including therapists and peripatetic staff so that they can all be aware of the plans and can offer support.

Stage 4 – Plan group and individual schemes of work to meet all aspects of students' needs.

Stage 5 – Plan assessment possibilities so that evidence of learning can . be considered (not rigidly decided) before activities are carried out.

Stage 6 – Implement plans and carry out the topic, assessing progress as you proceed.

Stage 7 – Evaluate the success of the topic and decide what has been learned with everyone involved.

It can be helpful to conceive of topics in seven stages (see previous page) and it is only when the sixth stage is reached that it is ready to carry out. Many people think that topic planning is a matter of drawing out the 'web' after which activities can begin. There is more to it than that.

Stage 4 often presents the biggest planning problems. How can you integrate basic learning into interesting and exciting topics, especially when each student's education programme is different? How can it all be rendered manageable so that teachers can meet the needs of every student in the group? Byers (1990) suggests using 'integrated schemes of work' through which students' individual objectives can be placed in natural and interesting contexts.

For example:

> Jenny needs to practise stretching out her arms to improve her motor abilities. She can do this in isolation with a suitable extrinsic reward but she can also stretch out to touch a rabbit as part of a topic on 'Pets' or bubbles as part of a topic on 'Water'. The possibilities are enormous.
>
> Ann and Bob are learning to write their names. There can be a wealth of drawings, models, games, tasks and activities that can be executed and labelled with names giving endless practice several times a day. This does not have to be an isolated exercise confined to English lessons.

The most important starting points are the basic needs of the students. The topics must be seen to serve these. However, it is remarkable how many basic learning needs can be given a natural context through careful choosing of topics such as 'Keeping Fit', 'Growing Vegetable Soup' and 'Running the Laundry'. Further information on running these particular topics can be found in:

Lacey, P. and Lomas, J. (1993) *Support Services and the Curriculum*. London: David Fulton Publishers.

Mount, H. and Ackerman, D. (1991) *Technology for All*. London: David Fulton Publishers.

Topics are great motivators. It is possible to keep the same basic learning needs through several different topics as the students slowly make their way towards competence and understanding. Topics are not just motivators for students but also for staff. This is particularly so for those who work with the most profoundly disabled students who may need years practising the same skills or developing basic understanding of the world around them. A new context for these is undoubtedly refreshing.

2. Reflection

Last session's focus

Begin your reflection by sharing with a partner or with the group an evaluation of the action plan that you made at the previous session. Was it successful? What did you learn? Where might you go next in this area?

This session's focus

Use the ideas that follow to guide small group discussion:

1. Draw a diagram of your existing curriculum structure. What are its strengths? What are its weaknesses?
    Does it serve the educational needs of the pupils? If the answer is a partial 'yes', make a list of the educational needs that are *not* met.
2. Make a list of the educational principles you think should be incorporated into curriculum design. As you proceed try to say why they are so important.

3. How To Move On

1. Discuss how the curriculum could better incorporate the principles you have described? Make a list of your ideas.
2. Discuss the ideas embodied in the examples presented in the Focus section of this Session and make a list of those aspects that you think will be helpful for your own curriculum development.
3. Decide on one subject to work on and take a small section relevant for one group of students. Apply changes to this section based on the results of your discussions.

4. Action Plan

Use this altered section for planning learning opportunities for the group of students over the next week.

Prepare to evaluate whether the new section has been an effective planning framework in terms of:

1. Demonstrating progress on a variety of learning dimensions.
2. Negotiating the learning path between student and teacher.
3. Responding to individual learning needs.
4. Recognising the value of process as well as product.
5. Responding to the integrated nature of the curriculum.

Further Reading

Reference	Points of Interest
Ainscow, M., Hopkins, D., Southworth, G. and West, M. (1994) *Creating Conditions for School Improvement. A Handbook of Staff Development Activities.* London: David Fulton Publishers.	Curriculum review
Byers, R. (1990) 'Topics: from myths to objectives', *British Journal of Special Education,* (17)3, 109-112.	Integrated schemes of work
Norwich, B. (1990) *Reappraising Special Needs Education.* London: Cassell.	Ends and means of teaching cannot be separated
Sebba, J., Byer, R. and Rose, R. (1993) *Redefining the Whole Curriculum for Pupils with Learning Difficulties.* London: David Fulton Publishers.	Curriculum design using interactive principles
Staff of Rectory Paddock School (1983) *In Search of a Curriculum.* Sidcup: Robin Wren Publications.	Curriculum for thinking skills

Principles of an interactive approach to curriculum design

- Valuing the process rather than the product.

- Importance of experiential learning.

- Negotiation between teacher and learner of the learning path.

- Importance of context and its relevance.

- Focus on developing the learners' *understandings* of the world around them.

- Flexibility to be responsive to the needs of individual learners.

- Broad and balanced enough to respond to a variety of different needs.

- Can be delivered in an integrated manner throughout the curriculum.

- Value of social interaction (relationships/PSE).

- Importance of student-centred active learning

- Motivation contained within the task rather than extrinsic to it.

- Value of a developmental progression in skills, understanding, knowledge and attitudes.

Interactive Approaches to Teaching. © Mark Collis and Penny Lacey

Developing the Curriculum

Phases of development	Key questions
Where are we now?	What is existing curriculum structure? Does it enable or obstruct learning? Does it enable the sort of learning we wish to encourage? How has it proven to be successful? What are its failings?
Where do we want to be?	What are the educational principles we hold dear?
How will we get there?	How can we incorporate these principles into our curriculum design? Do we want to adapt the existing structure to meet the requirements of these principles?
What do we want to do?	What is the school's vision? Precisely what changes to curriculum design do we want to make? What are its priorities for development? / what actually is possible?
Where will we go next?	Are we moving in the direction we wanted or have we been subtly 'red-herringed'? How can we keep the momentum going?

Adapted from Ainscow *et al.* (1994).

Interactive Approaches to Teaching. © Mark Collis and Penny Lacey

SESSION 10

Recording

An interactive view of recording challenges us to ask certain fundamental questions. It allows the opportunity to return to first principles and ask why and how we record. It is only from an analysis such as this that a useful system of recording may develop.

1. Focus

The following questions are intended to provoke the reader into a re-evaluation of the purposes of recording.

Question 1. Should we record the way in which students perform tasks rather than whether they can or cannot do them?

Interactive approaches encourage teachers to value the process of doing the task. Students' learning comes from the way tasks are performed as well as from end products and it is most valuable to focus recording on a description of this process. A recording system that simply encourages teachers to tick that skills have been acquired misses out on such a wealth of information which can be used to inform the next steps in teaching.

Record sheets may be designed to encourage comments to be written about how the task was performed.
Prompt questions might include:

- Did the student:
  - Take time to think about the problem?
  - Ask for help?
  - Involve other students in solving the problem?

A recording sheet might include these prompt questions with spaces for brief comments on what happened.

Question 2. Should recording concentrate on the implications of students' actions for wider tasks?

Interactive approaches may be considered essentially non-mechanistic. Teaching does not rely on the breaking down of the task into its sub-components. Instead, emphasis is placed on the wider picture and the context in which the learning takes place. Recording is therefore not restricted to a factual account of the achievement of these sub-steps. It can describe the relevance of the learning that has just taken place. The process of recording involves the making of a whole series of professional judgements, about how each piece of learning fits into students' lives. This issue has implications at all levels of recording, from individual task record sheets to termly summative reports.

Records should contain the implications of learning and achievement to the student. For example, the fact that John can independently heat a saucepan of milk may have a variety of implications for his life. Future learning can then be planned taking into account how this task was performed and what he may be able to build onto the skill.

There are occasions when it is important to report on the progress of individual sub-steps but the wider implications of this achievement must also be kept in mind. This issue is particularly relevant in the context of students with profound and multiple learning difficulties whose total learning is significantly limited and usually extremely slow. Recording for this group of students should be very careful to take into account both minute detail and overall direction.

Question 3. Should the process of recording involve the learner as well as the teacher whenever possible?

One of the features of an interactive approach is the negotiation of what is to be learned between students and teachers. Record keeping should have this same spirit of negotiation. A clear example of this may be seen in the principles of the records of achievement movement. Students are encouraged to discuss their achievements and the final result is an 'agreed record', rather than simply the teachers' interpretations of what the students know and can do.

Closely allied to this issue is that of ownership of the records. If learners are involved in the production of the record it really should become theirs. In the past there have been two kinds of records: records of achievement, to which students contribute; and teachers' records, to which they do not. In the future, it may be more appropriate for more records to incorporate the collaborative process. It cannot be overstated that the main reason for doing this would be to maximise the relevance, and therefore the usefulness of the information recorded.

Example record sheets in which students have been directly involved can be seen in Hazel Lawson's *Practical Record Keeping in Special Schools* (1993) and in the National Curriculum Council's *The National Curriculum and Children with Severe Learning Difficulties* (1993).

Question 4. How objective should records aspire to be?

To rely on purely factual accounts of students' behavioural responses will undoubtedly cause much useful information to be ignored. For example, if it is accepted that learning is contingent on the mood of the learner, then teachers will need to be aware of this aspect and although mood is notoriously difficult to assess objectively, records should contain information in this area.

Traditionally, teachers have been discouraged from being subjective on the basis that anything not directly observable is unprovable and relies on interpretation. In reality teachers have always made assumptions, drawing conclusions about what they feel concerning learning situations and how learners are responding. Objectivity is very difficult to achieve and recognising this can help to ensure that subjectivity is properly recognised and planned for. Attempting to decide whether a student understands a particular concept needs several examples of what the teacher considers to be demonstrations of understanding. These need to be offered as evidence to support subjective judgements.

Prompts for a record sheet for the excerpt of School A's curriculum used in Session 9 might contain:

Discrimination
Observe the level of understanding demonstrated by the student in natural situations. Record exactly what you judge to be the level of understanding of the concept of 'odd one out' or 'different'. Be specific with objects, circumstances, language, limitations. You will need several different examples as evidence.

Prompt:

1. Making sets (e.g. of kitchen utensils, clothes)

2. Pointing out differences in size, colour, shape etc. in ordinary conversation

3. Playing games when making sets is the object (e.g. Clock Patience or Snap)

4. Interchange of words such as 'different,' 'not the same,' 'odd,' 'not like'.

Question 5. Should what we record always be founded in evidence?

This question relates closely to the previous one. It is important to reach agreement about the nature of evidence. Is it purely what is seen and heard? If teachers adhere too much to the need for 'hard evidence' it is possible that the real purpose of recording (to inform what is taught next) can be forgotten in a desperate attempt to record what is seen.

It is worth asking, 'how is evidence of an interactive nature different from that of a behavioural nature?' One form of interactive evidence can be concerned with the quality of relationships. For example the process of getting to know students will mean that teachers can make inferences about what they understand and know. This may result from being in tune with the students and thus it may be difficult to provide hard evidence to support opinions.

Question 6. If learning is contingent on the quality of the relationship between the learner and the teacher, shouldn't we record details of the course of this relationship?

One of the most important aspects of interactive approaches is the recognition that learning takes place within the context of a relationship between teachers and learners (and between the students themselves). The quality and validity of the information that is recorded will largely be dependent on how well teachers know their students. Each member of a teaching team may record different information about learning because they are all at different stages in making a relationship with the student in question.

This diversity could be avoided through ensuring that only one person works with each student but this may be impractical or undesirable. An alternative is to include the relationship within the record. For example, a recorded comment might read, 'Michael's understanding of "one or more" was indicated by his eye contact with me, which I can interpret as pleasure in understanding a new concept.' This issue can easily be ignored, but at the cost of the value of what is recorded.

Question 7. How can a record reflect what has happened in the student's thought processes in, for instance, solving a problem?

Can records show how learners are thinking about strategies they may use to solve a particular problem? In reality these strategies will have to be verbalised or evidenced in some way to be recorded. For example, a record sheet might prompt the teacher into providing evidence that the learner was pondering different strategies, before acting on the problem with the chosen strategy.

In addition, how can the record demonstrate that a student has learned from using the wrong strategy to solve a problem? One way may be to study the way in which the task is performed on the next occasion, thereby showing that the student has thought about the mistake and does not do the same thing again.

It might be useful to look again at the Executive Control Task record sheet devised by the Staff at Rectory Paddock School summarised in Session 9 on page 97.

Question 8. Should records be as clear and concise as possible?

The thrust in this session has been towards a descriptive style of recording. Ticks in boxes cannot provide the amount of information necessary to plan meaningful learning experiences for students with learning difficulties. More detail is needed. However, if records should be more descriptive, conciseness becomes crucial. The description of how students completed tasks must be focused on what is *really* needed. Day-to-day recording can slip easily into becoming verbose, jargonised and unhelpful. It is vital continually to ask 'to what use are we going to put the statements we record?' If there is no use then why record it? Indeed, if no function is being served by a comment why write it down at all?

No doubt for the best of intentions many of us feel committed to record as fully as possible, particularly if this enables us to clarify our thoughts. This drive may perhaps be reinforced by a belief that this is what will satisfy OFSTED. But it is crucial that we are efficient in our recording and only record what is *useful.*

Question 9. How can we record and interact at the same time?

Writing records, when in the middle of a group activity, may be very difficult if not impossible. This is a very real, practical problem which relates to the management of recording. 'How can I both run a group that requires my input and record individual responses?' There are no easy answers, but it is an issue that must be tackled by teachers to ensure that records are more than just rushed jottings that are possible during class time, otherwise crucial bits of learning may be missed.

The following questions may be useful to promote discussion:

- In a class with more than one member of staff, can one be designated the sole task of recording at particular times?
- Can occasional sessions, or parts of sessions, be devoted to assessment?
- Can time be made available at the end of a session for recording to be completed with students?
- Can time be made available after the session for staff to get together?
- Can a regular record keeping meeting be held?
- Can record forms be designed for easy completion that can enable elaboration at a later date?
- Can another form of recording be considered? (e.g. video)

Discussions concerning manageability are very important as only when recording is manageable will it be effective.

Concluding Remarks

The effective management of recording is essential in the context of interactive teaching and those who are engaged in recording should actively think about how they can get the best out of the process. The following questions may be useful for discussion purposes:

- What do you record?
- When do you record?
- Who records? Who owns? Who has access?
- Who are you recording for?
- How will the record be managed?
- What will the record look like?

2. Reflection

Last Session's Focus

Begin your reflection by sharing with a partner or with the group an evaluation of the action plan that you made at the end of the previous session. Was it successful? What did you learn? Where might you go next in this area?

This Session's Focus

This session's focus has many questions embedded in the text. In pairs or small groups work through these using them to guide your discussion about your own school/centre's recording system.

3. How To Move On

1. With reference to the questions in the focus section, attempt to devise a record sheet suitable for use with a group for a specific activity. Choose a real group and a real activity so that trialling is possible.

2. Make sure that the issues featured in the focus are addressed within your record sheet.

4. Action Plan

Try out the record sheet you devised and evaluate it by asking the questions:

What have I recorded and how have I recorded it?

How can I use this for planning the next learning step?

Is there space for input from other professionals?

How well does the sheet actually work?

Is it clear?

Was it manageable?

Will it be manageable in the long term?

Does it record what I actually want it to record?

What improvements could be made?

Further Reading

Reference	Points of Interest
Lawson, H. (1993) *Practical Record Keeping in Special Schools.* London: David Fulton Publishers.	Examples of record sheets
National Curriculum Council (1993) *The National Curriculum and Children with Severe Learning Difficulties.* York: NCC.	Recording NC subjects
Nind, M. and Hewett, D. (1994) *Access to Communication,* London: David Fulton Publishers.	Recording NC subjects
Staff of Rectory Paddock School (1983) *In Search of a Curriculum.* Sidcup: Robin Wren Publications.	Recording thinking strategies

Record keeping

Question 1.   Should we record the ways in which students perform tasks rather than whether they can or cannot do them?

Question 2.   Should recording concentrate on the implications of students' actions for wider tasks?

Question 3.   Should the process of recording involve the learner as well as the teacher whenever possible?

Question 4.   How objective should records aspire to be?

Question 5.   Should what we record always be founded in evidence?

Question 6.   If learning is contingent on the quality of the relationship between the learner and the teacher, shouldn't we record details of the course of this relationship?

Question 7.   How can a record reflect what has happened in the student's thought processes in, for example, solving a problem?

Question 8.   Should records be as clear and concise as possible?

Question 9.   How can we record and interact at the same time?

Interactive Approaches to Teaching. © Mark Collis and Penny Lacey

Conclusion

This book was born from a frustration with traditional techniques for teaching students with learning difficulties and also from the results of a survey in a group of teachers anxious to know more about alternatives. The search for 'something more ...' is undoubtedly a useful process in itself, but it can prove time consuming and frustrating for busy practitioners. It has been the aim of this text to guide that search. We have tried to challenge you to reconsider your existing teaching practices through a process of returning to principles. We have attempted to explore the implications of interactive approaches to teachers and students in a way that will really affect practice.

Our aim has been to guide your professional development through a process of examining the way in which theory and practice come together. This has been placed within an in-service training framework to encourage groups of professionals to discuss implications for their own work. The issues we have explored (for example the relevance of interactive approaches for recording) are ones that will affect how teachers work in classrooms the next day. Workplace-based training can be a powerful means through which proposed change can be debated and supported.

The text was intended to challenge you to reflect on your teaching and it will not be surprising if it leads you to ask further questions. There is, of course, no one way to 'do interactive approaches' and this was not intended to be a recipe book with step-by-step guidance. We hope that you will follow up some of the references to deepen your knowledge and understanding of the implications of interactive approaches to teaching.

Appendix

How to Start Doing Intensive Interaction

Dave Hewett

Intensive interaction is a way of teaching communication before speech. A way of using yourself, your face, voice, body and personality as the main teaching resource for helping people with very severe learning difficulties to learn more about giving attention to other people and taking part in communicative interactions.

Preparing

Don't rush anything you do; the idea is to adapt your behaviour to the preferred tempo of life of the student and have a great time yourself while doing it. Enjoyment of what is taking place, yours and the student's, should be present at all times during interactive sessions. It is okay to enjoy yourself during our work and it is right for the student that she or he learns this way.

Be sensitive at all times to student signalling. 'Student signalling' implies all means by which the person may intentionally or unintentionally give messages about feelings, thoughts, preferences, desires etc. This can be by use of face, voice body language, position in room, or emotional atmosphere. This skill or process has been termed 'tuning-in' to the student.

Also part of tuning-in is to start a process of familiarisation with the student's behaviour which will enable you to be knowledgeable about things the person does, moods, feelings, etc. and the way in which the student signals these things. A good way of starting work using this approach is to do observations, even if you already know the person quite well. Give yourself opportunities for watching the person enjoyably. These observations can be quite subjective, with no attempt to do anything other than become as familiar as possible with the student's facial expressions, movements and body language.

You are working towards using yourself as a sensitive interactive partner to the student to create interactive play situations where the basis for the activities is first of all the quality of the way that **you** respond to what the student does.

Thus the activities for which you are preparing are highly 'student centred' owing to your sensitivity to student behaviour and sensibilities. The 'content' of the activities is primarily formed by your preparedness to use student behaviour and sensibilities as the focus for what takes place. This is known as the principle and technique of 'follow/use' student behaviour.

Follow/use is **the** principle and technique which is most central to doing Intensive Interaction. If you like, you will be setting up joint sessions with the student where the idea is that you pleasurably respond to aspects of the student's behaviour, and celebrate them to create the activity between you. The emphasis should be on responsiveness and a relaxed tempo, rather than you, the teacher, controlling and driving along everything which takes place. In fact, one of the basics of using the approach successfully is that you hold back your behaviour to create time, space and security for the student to produce behaviour to which you respond.

Be prepared to allow yourself to use various aspects of your intellect and personality to tune in and be responsive. Most teachers seem to find that it is possible to work interactively by intellectual understanding and use of the principles and techniques, but that in various ways they also use and combine this with less rational means of behaving, where they start to behave intuitively, with less intellectual thought governing their responses during interactions. There seem to be variations about the extent to which individual teachers do this; some claim to work entirely naturally, giving little conscious thought to what they are about to do next.

As an inevitable aspect of the follow/use principle, be prepared for Intensive Interaction activities to take place in a variety of locations according to the individual preference of the student on that day, or at that time. Be prepared too for the activity not to take place at all if the student does not wish it or is merely inexplicably unresponsive that day.

Rather, it is your responsibility to 'promote' the activity by the use of enjoyment as the prime motivator, by making the activities enjoyable and 'right' for the students, by your preparedness to centre the activities on the students' behaviour and sensibilities and by your preparedness to allow yourself to play and enjoy yourself and the company of the student to the full. For some teachers, there is reason to believe that this sense of immersed and tuned-in playfulness is more effective at promoting the responsive teacher style than rational and technical knowledge. If you feel that it will be difficult to tune-in and achieve this state of mutual enjoyment with a particular student, pause and take stock of the situation.

Any difficulty you may feel you are experiencing in enjoying being with this person needs to be addressed. You may need to discuss the situation with colleagues and spend some time observing a colleague with this student who does not share your reservations about this person. The idea is that by observing this member of staff, you will start to see aspects of the student's personality which have previously been denied to you because of the level of your reservations about enjoying being with this person. It is essential to effective interaction that there is a great deal of unhindered mutual enjoyment present and a degree of emotional empathy or 'warmth'.

Starting

All things being well, you can think about starting activities. Be prepared to go to where the person is, particularly if she or he has a preferred room or place in a room which offers the greatest sense of security and familiarity. Be prepared also to interact on the move if the student is a person who indulges in a great deal of physical activity. Use your face, voice and body language to transmit signals of 'availability' and enjoyment.

Assume a physical position which enables you to signal the above and which also best fosters a face-to-face orientation or the potential for it, if the student should choose to look at your face. Even if face-to-face contact is not made, find a position which best enables the exchange of signals of all types. Be prepared to work in a variety of different physical positions, often not on a chair at a table.

Be prepared to use physicality liberally. Use of touch seems to be important in these activities. It is reasonable to suppose that touch will be an important channel of communication for people with limited communication ability, as long as the person wants to touch and be touched. Your use of touch can vary between – at one extreme – simple low-intensity patting or stroking to – at the other extreme – high activity romping with extensive body contact. Advice on safeguards for use of physical contact is included at the end of this chapter.

Find a situation and a position where the student is tolerating your presence (at the very least your presence should be tolerated; if it isn't then go back even further into probably slow, sensitive work aimed at enabling the student to develop basic tolerance of your presence). Start to look for things which the person does to which you can respond with the intention of starting to interact, or at its most simple, share. Focus jointly and then start to take turns in exchanges of behaviour developed from the joint focus.

Responding to the Student

You can now take opportunities to respond to behaviours of the student which you select as offering an enjoyable potential starting point of mutual focus. This may also be the starting point for what can be called a chain of causality that is, taking turns in an exchange of behaviours where each person's turn of behaviour is related contingently to the other person's previous turn. Put simply, you are aiming to achieve this thought for the student, 'I do something'. Because of that she does something. Because of that I do something, and so on. Enabling the student to start thinking in this way and enjoying the experimentations that go with it that create turn-taking dialogues is one of the most basic intentions of doing Intensive Interaction.

Do not forget at any point the need to maintain enjoyment and positivity in the interactions. A golden rule for the early stages is to respect any signal of negativity from the student by immediately either stopping or pausing in what you are doing or by modifying your input with the intention of getting everything back to positive again.

For the teacher, there are two methods of responding which can promote chains of causality or contingent turn-taking. These have been called 'response scenarios'. Both scenarios seem straightforward in method, but other teacher abilities such as sensitivity, intuition, playfulness and timing have a bearing on their successful use.

Scenario 1

Simply relax and watch and wait for the student to do something which appeals to you as being something to which you would like to respond. The selection or decision-making process you use can be influenced by intellectual preferences, or emotional ones, or both simultaneously. You may do things without having a pre-planning rational reason for doing it. The behaviour or aspect of the person that you select for response should be something that you will find interesting and enjoyable as a focus for play activity. There are a variety of ways in which you can make your response something that the other person may find interesting (examples listed below). You do not have to concentrate on any one behaviour or aspect of the person and can feel free to experiment with your responses to a variety of things that the person does, bearing in mind always the need for that person to feel secure and to be enjoying your presence. Be alert to respond again if your response causes a further response from the student.

Scenario 2

Attempt to initiate a turn-taking exchange by taking the first turn with the intention of promoting or providing a pleasurable response from the student, by doing something which is designed to be attractive or interesting or amusing or significant to that person. Your decision as to what you do may well be based on good judgement as a result of your tuning-in so far, or it will be possible that you will do something based upon tuning-in, but with less rational planning. It simply 'felt' like a good thing to do. If you succeed in obtaining a pleasurable response from the student to what you did, be alert to respond immediately to the student's response, and to the further possibility that the student will respond a second time, in response to you.

Suggestions for ways of responding to student behaviours: Scenario 1

1. Enjoyably imitate or copy something that the student is doing at that moment, but continue to scrutinise carefully to be sure that the person enjoys what you are doing.

2. Join in with what the student is doing. Find a way of interweaving your behaviour with that of the student so that you are enjoyably sharing a focus which is centred on what the student likes doing. Stereotyped behaviours can often be an enjoyable focus for joining-in, but again scrutinise to be sure that the person is enjoying this type of attention. Use gentle tease, for instance, playfully denying access to a favoured object or activity, but again you must pay utmost attention to the gentleness of the tease and signals of continuing enjoyment from the student. Tease can be used frequently and

successfully if this sensitivity is observed.

3. Respond with a dramatised behaviour. This means that any behaviour you might use which is playfully dramatic has the intention of making your behaviour significant thus attracting the attention of the student.

4. Respond with running commentary. Use your voice to make a response to what has just taken place. This is intended to be significant and attract the attention of the student. This does not imply that use of voice should be restricted only to moments when you are attempting to 'win' significant attention from the student.

5. Combination of 1 to 4. Frequently the difference between, for instance, imitating something which the student is doing and joining-in with it may not be clear. It may be that you are doing both. Another example may be that you use running commentary fairly continuously, so that if part of your running commentary is to comprise the significant response, then at that moment you dramatise the running commentary. A sensation of overlap between these ways of responding, of them blending into each other, is to be expected and is good technique. Once more, you may have the sensation of not fully controlling these response with the overlap occurring seemingly naturally.

Suggestions for ways of initiating: Scenario 2 (Figure A.1)

You can offer, as the first behaviour in a potential exchange of turn-taking, virtually anything which you judge, based on the knowledge you have about the person from tuning-in, that the person might find significant – amusing or stimulating in some manner. These are a few examples:

- tickling
- stroking
- patting
- other physical contact
- use of voice
- use of posture
- a movement
- a facial expression
- a combination of several of the above.

An often used and effective style of taking the first turn is to use 'burst-pause'. Burst-pause is a style of teacher behaviour which is aimed at producing a response from the student, and therefore offers to the student a significant teacher behaviour in a manner which is highly suggestive of a response from the student. Burst-pause is characteristically as follows:

1. The teacher produces the behaviour which is intended to produce the response in a short burst, up to about 2 seconds.

2. The teacher immediately pauses; stills or virtually stills her or his behaviour. The pause is usually shorter than the burst. The teacher maintains

signalling using body language and facial expression which sends the message of expectation that there will be a response.

3. Teacher repeats (1) and (2) up to say, five times until a response (which can be responded to) is forthcoming, or the teacher judges that this initiation will not work in terms of producing a response.

Types of student response

These are examples of the sorts of student behaviour usually sought as a response, or as a behaviour which can be interpreted as a response:

- smiles/signs of pleasure
- other facial expressions
- eye contact
- laughter
- sounds, especially pleasurable ones
- Looking at the teacher's face
- Looking in the direction of the teacher's face
- body position body movements.

Additional considerations

When using burst-pause, the overall sensation or atmosphere generated by your behaviour should be relaxed playfulness, even though you are adopting behaviour which has the intention of obtaining a response from the student.

You can help the student to learn responsiveness by clever use of your responses. A good technique frequently seen is for the teacher to respond to student behaviours which are not responses, with significant behaviour which pretends that the student behaviour was a response. Consistent use of this technique can help the student to understand that her or his behaviour can have significant effect on the behaviour of other people.

Some teachers operate this pretence fully, interpreting the student's behaviours whilst interacting as being wholly meaningful or interpretable as intentional, even if the behaviour is clearly not fully meaningful. The extent to which teachers employ this mental process varies from individual to individual.

Pause – varying the intensity of activities

Interaction activities, when up and running, rarely continue at one level of intensity. Indeed, they are more successful, particularly during the early stages, if you respect the student's ability to participate for a short period of seconds. Even as the student becomes more adept at taking part and is an entirely motivated contributor, there will still be a need for this person to 'rest' briefly during sequences, and a teacher skill is to be able to be sensitive to these needs, recognise the signals from the student and respond immediately by pausing completely until the student is able to start again.

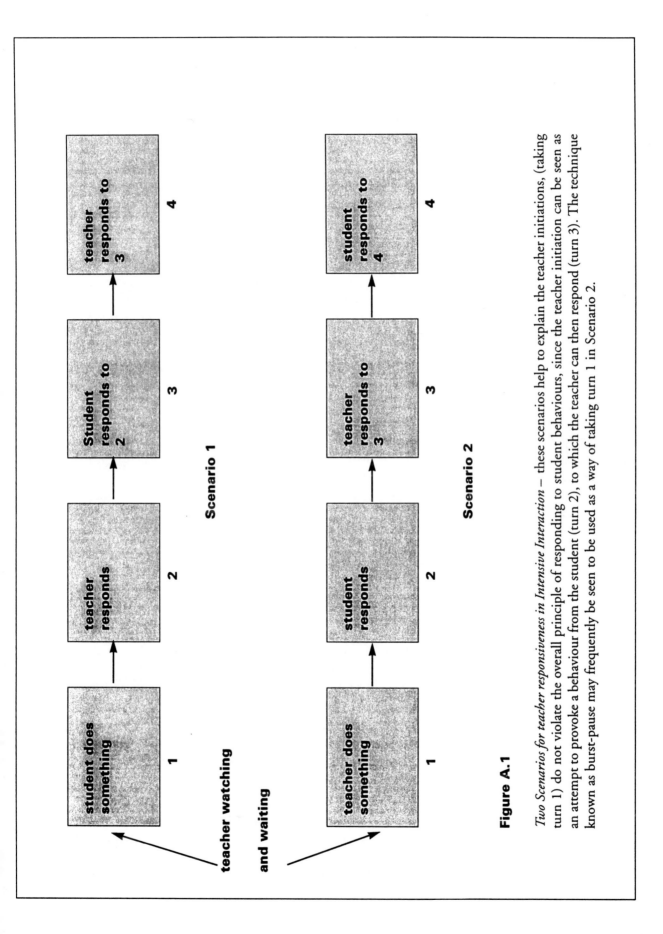

Figure A.1

Two Scenarios for teacher responsiveness in Intensive Interaction – these scenarios help to explain the teacher initiations, (taking turn 1) do not violate the overall principle of responding to student behaviours, since the teacher initiation can be seen as an attempt to provoke a behaviour from the student (turn 2), to which the teacher can then respond (turn 3). The technique known as burst-pause may frequently be seen to be used as a way of taking turn 1 in Scenario 2.

Once one activity of shared or exchanged behaviour with you and the student participating effectively is established, exploit it and repeat it several times daily. This is the first stage of the growth of that person's repertoire of such activities. You can now expect to widen this repertoire by these means:

1. Attempt to capitalise on different aspects of the student's behaviour by further use of watching and waiting and Response Scenario 1. Establish these activities as part of the repertoire by the same process as above.

2. Continually repeat, practise and rehearse activities from the repertoire. This continuous repetition is in itself a force for forward progress and growth in communicative activities as the repetitions have the potential to generate variations and divergences.

3. Thus, widen the variety of activities by facilitating the development of new and different activities by capitalising on variations from existing ones.

4. Use teamwork. From the earliest possible stages it is desirable, if not essential, that there is more than one interactive partner for each student. This enables the student to benefit both from the differences and from the similarities in input between the two members of staff. It also enables the student to generalise newly formed skills and knowledge as early as possible and the staff should benefit from joint collusion and evaluation.

Use of physical contact in work with people with learning disabilities – guidelines for safeguards

- *Know why you do it* – Be knowledgeable on the purposes of using physical contact by discussion, thought and by reading the pertinent psychological and developmental literature.

- *Have consent from the person* – Obey the usual conventions governing physical contact with another person. If you rarely get consent to touch, then go back a few stages and work toward obtaining willingly given consent. At the very least, physical contact may be necessary to carry out basic care.

- *Be prepared to discuss and explain your practice* – First and foremost by being knowledgeable, as above.

- *Document. Have it acknowledged in the school curriculum document or workplace brochure* – The culture and working practices of the school or other workplace are acknowledged in the curriculum document or workplace brochure and this will include explication of the use of physical contact and the purposes of it.

- *Document. Have it acknowledged in any individual programme for the person* – Be assertive. If you are certain that use of physical contact is fulfilling the person's needs educationally or developmentally, then state this in the documentation drawn up to support work with that person.

- *Have good teamwork, both organisational and emotional* – Teamworking practices should literally facilitate staff working together in teams so that staff or students are rarely alone. The teamworking ethos should also include good discussions among staff concerning the emotional aspects of the work including, crucially, orientations toward the issue of use of physical contact.

- *Use of physical contact should be discussed openly and regularly* – There should be no sense of furtiveness or 'hidden curriculum'. This important aspect of teaching technique should tangibly be a matter of open discussion and study.

- *Have others present* – The most basic safeguard for staff and students is to have other staff present in the room when in situations where physical contact is likely to be used.

Further Reading

Nind, M. and Hewett, D. (1994) *Access to Communication: Developing the Basics of Communication with People with Severe Learning Difficulties Through Intensive Interaction*. London: David Fulton Publishers.

Index